WISH I WERE HERE

OUTSPOKEN

Series editors: Adrian Parr and Santiago Zabala

Pointed, engaging, and unafraid of controversy, books in this series articulate the intellectual stakes of pressing cultural, social, environmental, economic, and political issues that unsettle today's world. Outspoken books are disruptive: they shake things up, change how we think, and make a difference. The Outspoken series seeks above all originality of perspective, approach, and thought. It encourages the identification of novel and unexpected topics or new and transformative approaches to inescapable questions, whether written from within established disciplines or from viewpoints beyond disciplinary boundaries. Each book brings theoretical inquiry into a reciprocally revealing encounter with material realities and lived experience. This series tackles the complex challenges faced by societies the world over, rethinking politics, justice, and social change in the twenty-first century.

WISH
I WERE
HERE

Boredom and
the Interface

MARK KINGWELL

McGill-Queen's University Press

Montreal & Kingston • London • Chicago

© McGill-Queen's University Press 2019

ISBN 978-0-7735-5712-3 (cloth)
ISBN 978-0-7735-5793-2 (ePDF)
ISBN 978-0-7735-5794-9 (ePUB)

Legal deposit first quarter 2019
Bibliothèque nationale du Québec

Printed in Canada on acid-free paper

This book has been published with the help of a grant from the Canadian Federation
for the Humanities and Social Sciences, through the Awards to Scholarly Publications
Program, using funds provided by the Social Sciences and Humanities Research Council
of Canada.

We acknowledge the support of the Canada Council for the Arts, which last year invested
$153 million to bring the arts to Canadians throughout the country.

Nous remercions le Conseil des arts du Canada de son soutien. L'an dernier, le Conseil
a investi 153 millions de dollars pour mettre de l'art dans la vie des Canadiennes et des
Canadiens de tout le pays.

Library and Archives Canada Cataloguing in Publication

Kingwell, Mark, 1963–, author
Wish I were here : boredom and the interface / Mark Kingwell.

(Outspoken)
Includes bibliographical references and index.
Issued in print and electronic formats.
ISBN 978-0-7735-5712-3 (hardcover).–ISBN 978-0-7735-5793-2 (ePDF).–
ISBN 978-0-7735-5794-9 (ePUB)

1. Technology–Philosophy. I. Title.

T14.K56 2019   601   C2018-906525-7   C2018-906526-5

It can't be helped: boredom is not simple. We do not escape boredom (with a work, a text) with a gesture of impatience or rejection. Just as the pleasure of the text supposes a whole indirect production, so boredom cannot presume it is entitled to any spontaneity: there is no sincere boredom: if the prattle-text bores me personally, it is because in reality I do not like the demand. But what if I did like it (if I had some maternal appetite)? Boredom is not far from bliss: it is bliss seen from the shores of pleasure.

Roland Barthes, *Le Plaisir du texte* (1973)

WOOLWORTH BUILDING, NEW YORK.

CONTENTS

PREFACE

A certain amount of boredom is essential to a happy life.

Bertrand Russell, *The Conquest of Happiness* (1930)

In 1999 the English artist Martin Parr published a book that became an unlikely bestseller and coffee-table or desk essential. *Boring Postcards* was exactly what its title promised: a chunky album of 160 images drawn from Parr's personal collection of the dullest imaginable scenes and features of British life.[1] Unremarkable railway stations, brick-faced factory buildings, empty interiors, motel rooms, hotel lounges, sad post offices, and bleak stretches of motorway all found a place in this eerie celebration of the mundane and vapid. Many people found the book hilarious; some considered it sad. Nobody seemed to find it at all boring – on the contrary, in fact.

And yet, the images within the covers most certainly are of dull scenes and insignificant structures, however useful in achieving the ends of ordinary life. For me, as for many others, the book seemed at once revelatory and familiar. Like other examples of found art or aesthetic repurposing of ordinary things, it offered what Arthur Danto has called "the transfiguration of the commonplace." We see here the banality of so much of the built environment, as well as the poignancy of our need to connect and communicate. Why would anyone, we wonder, choose a parking lot or a turnpike entrance as the subject of a picture postcard? Humans are visible in some of the scenes, but many of them are blank of life, neutron-bombed scenes of empty everydayness. They illustrate the tedium of daily life even as they play with the fashionable notion of "folk photography" – the repositioning of trivial images to shine a bright light on their routine but profound longing. Parr added no commentary or theory, simply allowing the images to speak for themselves.

When Parr added a companion volume of American postcards in 2000 (*Boring Postcards USA*) and of German ones in 2001 (*Langweilige Postkarten*), the project ascended to new heights. Now vaster highways, toll booths, airports, border crossings, high-rise apartments, empty swimming pools, and suburban subdivisions joined the array of vapid surroundings. Flipping through these books, especially *Boring Postcards USA*, creates a visual version of the road-trip sections of Nabokov's *Lolita* (1955), in which Humbert Humbert's sour catalogue of neon-lit roadside diners, chain groceries, burger stands, gas stations, and motels becomes a mounting polemic against postwar America and its vacuous, enervating prosperity. Parr is never so judgmental. Once again there is a celebratory feeling to this collection, yet tinged with sadness. Having a great time, wish you were here! No, really I *wish you were here*, because being here without you means I am less than myself.

Postcards have been with us for a long time, but one of the most intense crazes for them came about a century ago, when it was extremely fashionable to send lithographed scenes of life on the road to friends and family left behind. One of my favourite pieces of ephemera is a postcard of the Woolworth Building in New York (1912), which I found some years ago in a New Hampshire barn. A wavy line of fountain-pen ink marks the pinnacle of the towering structure. "Was up this last winter," the script notes for the information of those still on the farm. Even the hues of the early picture postcard become a familiar palette, of pale tones and comic-book print quality, such that later ones, from the 1970s on, have a glossy, lustrous finish that seems incongruous and somehow wrong.

Meanwhile, at the same time as people were sending millions of penny postcards, cheap and portable photographic equipment made it possible for amateurs to capture "real-photo" images and share the results, in small print runs, with their communities: Instagram for the Industrial Age. Millions of postcards, many of them as luminously boring as anything in Parr's collections, were fabricated and sent between 1905 and 1912, the peak postcard craze.[2]

A postcard is not merely an image, however, and that is one reason I have used postcards as a visual accompaniment to the text that follows. They tell a story of selfhood in search of itself. Postcards are elements within large systems – of cities and towns and farms, of postal and printing services, of tourist trade and vacations, and of family, friends, and co-workers. The image is really just the occasion, or the carrier, for creating a tiny node of personal signal within the vastness of this web of collective and communicative action. The message on the back is likewise secondary to the fact of the postcard's being sent. Indeed, as anyone who has browsed in a Sunday flea market will know, many postcards contained no written message at all, just an address. The sought-for connection was the real freight.

This is a book about our seeking such connections, and the dangers and opportunities contained within that network of desire. The *boring* postcard offers several important insights. The first is that the boring postcard is not actually boring. There is a dynamic here, whereby we first register the trite or bland image, finding it somehow incredible, then move on to an appreciation of the image that is the opposite of boring and is, we could likewise say, the opposite of the nostalgia often aroused by old mail. Then there is a subsequent moment of ironic doubling, holding both previous ideas in a delicious tension. Funny? Yes. Sad? Also yes. Fascinating? Absolutely. The boring postcard thus gives us, in visual form, something of a hint about how boredom might function more generally – or, to be more precise, how we might come to appreciate boredom in ways that are philosophically interesting. Cultivating that appreciation is the main purpose of this book.

There is a second insight here, concerning what I am calling the Interface. Because we live in a world dominated by technology, and also because I focus on many technological details in my discussion, there is a tendency to think of interfaces as exclusively aspects of the computer age. Worse, there is a tendency to collapse the notion of interface to a specific platform or program. As I argue in what follows, even computer interfaces are more than this: they embrace the user, the user experience, even the tactile elements of time spent with specific programs (swiping, clicking, thumb-typing, etc.). More expansively, the Interface embraces social, political, and economic factors that are all in play in late-capitalist life, from the material conditions and routine immiseration that enabled the device in our hands or on our desks, to the psychological and spiritual conditions shaping the time we spend with them.

In still larger terms, the Interface is an apt description of many non-tech elements of human existence. I mean simple things like thresholds, doorways, windows, and passageways, which are essential to moulding the various affordances of work and home. I also mean more complex features of interaction, bordering, and passing through, such as the very turnpikes, departure lounges, parking lots, and motel rooms that feature prominently in Parr's catalogue of boringness. These are interstitial spaces, where we are not quite ourselves, suspended on the way to something that the postcard hints at but never depicts. Boredom is about getting stuck, feeling frustration at being so stuck, and feeling acutely that one does not want to be stuck ever again. The boring postcard depicts the *scene of boredom* as well-being itself, at least at first glance, boring.

One of the more extended examples in the book is Heidegger's celebrated discussion of boredom while stuck at a train station. Today we might instead focus on an airport or bus station, with seemingly endless bouts of tedium somehow never quite alleviated by all efforts to combat them, including free Wi-Fi connections and distracting mini shopping malls. These attractions lose any possible savour because we are there only in order to go somewhere else. The airport in particular is, we might say, the neoliberal train station. By definition a nowhere-zone, a utopia in the literal sense, it is a non-location where nothing happens and nothing can be done. Effort is pointless and frustration never far away. The only point of an airport is our leaving it behind.[3] Matters lie just the same with the scattered hotels and motels of life, those anonymous and temporary rooms where we stop for the night. These rooms, so often depressing in their anonymity and sameness, are Interfaces too. Structured and even comfortable, they find us forever stuck on the way to something else. Postcards sent from such places, *depicting* such places, are particularly poignant in their interstitial boringness.

Sometimes the abbreviated stall of a hotel becomes more permanent. There is the shower stall at the Bates Motel in Alfred Hitchcock's *Psycho* (1960), where Marion Crane (Vivien Leigh), on the lam with the gains from a bank heist, is cut down by jittery, mother-obsessed Norman Bates (Anthony Perkins).[4] There is the slick Hotel California of the Eagles' greatest hit (1976), with its pink champagne on ice and the weird affliction of "Mercedes bends," a hostelry where you can check out any time you want but – spoiler alert! – *you can never leave*. Appositely, critics of social-platform design sometimes refer to the "Hotel California" effect embedded in design features that make leaving a site difficult: a central target of my discussion in what follows.[5] We are stuck in the Interface, beguiled by our own device-imprisonment.

Perhaps most vividly, young engineering student Hans Castorp travels to a deluxe sanatorium in Thomas Mann's *The Magic Mountain* (1924), intending to stay for three days and ultimately spending seven spellbound years. This even though he does not in fact suffer from the tuberculosis that the clear mountain air of the sanatorium is supposed to aid. Castorp is never precisely bored as the days and month flow by, but his time atop the mountain is somehow boring in a vague generalized sense of the pointlessness of contented indolence. Why can't he just *do* something? Time itself, Mann suggests, expands and contracts according to our moods and conditions. What, after all, is seven years? Castorp has found that the in-between space of temporary dwelling suits him as a permanent condition. In other people, the very same outward condition might generate insanity.

But there is one further hotel where permanent enclosure is a danger, and it is directly relevant to the business of writing philosophy. In 1962 the Hungarian Marxist philosopher György Lukács used the image of "The Grand Hotel Abyss" to criticize his fellow theorists for their comfortable laziness in tenured academic posts. "A considerable part of the leading German intelligentsia, including Adorno, have taken up residence in the 'Grand Hotel Abyss,'" he wrote, "which I described in connection with my critique of Schopenhauer as 'a beautiful hotel, equipped with every comfort, on the edge of an abyss, of nothingness, of absurdity. And the daily contemplation of the abyss between excellent meals or artistic entertainments, can only heighten the enjoyment of the subtle comforts offered.'"[6] We lose ourselves in comfort, Lukács suggests, even as we try to fool ourselves and others that we are engaged in rigorous critical work. I am rather more charitable about Adorno than Lukács, perhaps, but the main argument holds. The point of philosophy, as Marx famously said, is to change the world, not merely interpret it.

Before getting on with what I hope might prove some small example of that kind of philosophy, a small coincidence is worth mentioning. Thomas Mann was Lukács's favourite author, defended at length in the latter's voluminous literary criticism. In fact, the Hungarian philosopher was reputedly a model for Leo Naphta, the austere Jewish-Jesuit-Marxist intellectual who dominates Castorp's intellectual world, endlessly arguing with the hedonistic humanist Luigi Settembrini. (Naphta later kills himself in a duel with the Italian.) Naphta is far more *dégagé* and cynical than Lukács, who joined Imre Nagy's anti-Soviet government as a Cabinet minister in 1956, and as a result endured threats of execution and deportation to Romania.

And finally, a word about moods. All writing conveys a mood, it seems to me, and sometimes it shifts over the course of a book. A mood, as Heidegger reminds us, is no simple psychological state or species of affect. Moods express how we find ourselves in the world, how we are living and faring.[7] They are a fundamental part of how humans have a world. I am always therefore in some mood or other. Moods both condition and reflect the world as we find it, how we stand with ourselves and the world together. They are indispensable to human existence, to understanding our existence and our prospects. And so I offer, in the pages that follow, a running status update on the dominant moods found in each of the four sections of this book. These updates may or may not prove illuminating to the reader, but I offer them in the spirit of sharing one of the conditions of any book's possibility – and one whose importance is too often denied or occluded, especially in academic writing. Books are written by humans, after all. Most of them, anyway …

WISH I WERE HERE

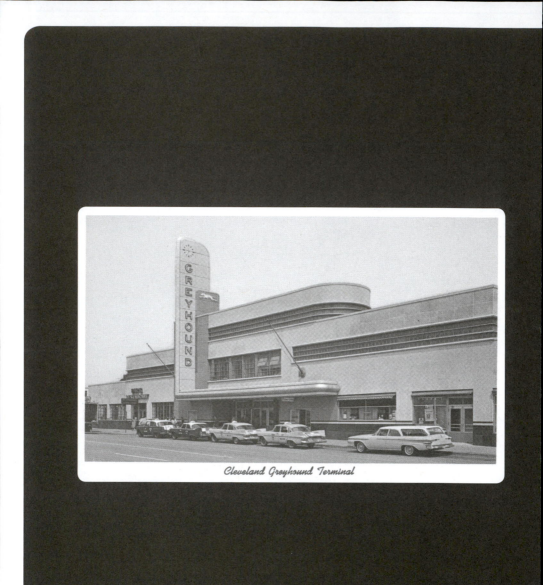

Cleveland Greyhound Terminal

PART ONE
THE CONDITION

MOOD REPORT

eerie,

restless,

frustrated

Life, friends, is boring. We must not say so.

John Berryman, "Dream Song 14" (1969)

Never yet, however, has the case been heard of in philosophy where a bland triviality did not conceal behind it the abyssal difficulty of the problem.

Martin Heidegger, *The Fundamental Concepts of Metaphysics* (1929–30)

Boredom is one of the most common of human experiences, yet it seems continually to defy complete understanding. We all know what it is to feel bored, but what exactly prompts, constitutes, or follows from the condition of boredom is far less obvious. Is boredom a function of leisure, such that there was, as some critics have argued, no such thing as boredom before, say, the age of Schopenhauer? Or is medieval *accidie* perhaps the appropriate forebear, tinged with sinfulness as well as the routine despair of not wanting to do anything in particular? Does boredom tangle desire, or personal conditions, or both? That is, when I stare at the full refrigerator and complain that there is nothing to eat, or when I scan a hundred cable channels and find nothing to watch, who or what, exactly, is to blame?

No surprise, then, that there are many intellectual accounts of the condition of boredom, or its cognates. This includes both a distinguished philosophical mini-tradition running from (at least) Schopenhauer and Kierkegaard through Heidegger to Adorno, and a lively recent psychological literature about the "creative" possibilities of boredom.[1] There is, likewise, a recurrent concern within contemporary discourse about technology and culture about the perils of boredom, how it can be identified and addressed by various instruments, and why this is presumptively necessary.

In all previous models of boredom, whether the ultimate conclusion was positive or negative, the self in question is presumed stable and available to experience. That is, whether we seek boredom, fear it, domesticate it, or revile it, the philosophical status of the implied subjects of boredom is mostly opaque *because it is presupposed to be already understood.* Even in these accounts, perhaps especially in Heidegger and the psychoanalytic literature, there is a sense that this will not entirely do: boredom is not so much a feature of the given landscape as of the figure confronting, or simply finding itself within, the landscape.

What does boredom reveal about fractured or spectral subjectivity and its relation to happiness? A century ago, modernist poets and artists worked to illustrate the disintegrated selfhood of twentieth-century humanity, the way a coherent individuality was being torn apart by new social and political conditions such that we were left with, at best, fragments shored against our ruin. Today the challenge is urgent in a new fashion, since our selves are deliberately scattered data-fragments – Twitter feeds, Instagram posts, shopping preferences, and text-trends captured by algorithms that seem to know us better than we know ourselves. What hope is there for integration and stability under such conditions? And, even more to the present point, what's boredom got to do with it? We can begin to flesh out an answer by categorizing more precisely the different accounts of the condition of boredom. Or I should say "conditions," because one obvious initial insight here is that the experience in play may be quite different, depending on the theoretical framework used to critique or (less often) celebrate it. As always, we must be aware that conceptual schemes, especially methodological ones, exist in order to produce the sort of results they are themselves fashioned to pick out.

But all of us, at least in the richer parts of the planet where stimulus is rich, are aware of the problem. I am sitting in front of a screen. I have a Netflix show playing, which I interrupt every few minutes to check my email in response to a little tune indicating an incoming message. If it is the right time of day, there is a muted baseball game showing on the nearby TV. I have my phone on the desk, which relentlessly delivers voicemail messages about daily trivia from people I know. I answer some of them. A web browser window is open in another tab, in case I want to fact-check something without troubling my failing memory, order a book I almost forgot on Amazon, or suddenly feel like wandering down a hot-link tunnel of scant and certainly forgettable relevance to what I still call my life. I can't settle to any one thing, let alone walk away from the light cast by the screens into a different reality. I am troubled, restless, overstimulated. I am consuming myself as a function of the attention I bestow. I am a zombie self, a spectre, suspended in a vast framework of technology and capital allegedly meant for my comfort and entertainment. And yet, and yet … I cannot find myself here.

For what it's worth, and as fair warning about my own biases in the following discussion, and despite occasional fits of media-saturation, I should just say that I actually am some species of neo-Luddite. I engage in no Facebook, Twitter, or Instagram activity. I have a Twitter account – but with zero tweets. I do not text. Like Bartleby the Scrivener, I would prefer not to. I have an aggressively low-tech flip phone that nobody but a child of the 1960s would consider "smart," though I consider it so in the fashion-magazine sense of the word. Even my parents spend more time online than I do. I realize that this is not the way most people live today, or want to live. But that is the point of the present argument. There is no special virtue in my tiny refusals, naturally. They are just middle-aged tics or forms of academic eccentricity in sanctioned twenty-first-century form. The neo-Luddite lifestyle choice is forever revealed as a reverse-polarity luxury good, in a general luxury-good economy of rampant plenitude.

Boredom, especially the species of it that I am going to label "neoliberal," depends for its force on the workings of an attention economy in which we are mostly willing participants. In the form of pervasive distraction and proffered connection or communication, social media and other online mechanisms act to harvest our attention. Sites are rated for number of hits, or stickiness, while those from whom the attention is reaped congratulate themselves on likes, retweets, and high numbers of friends or followers. In all these acts we do the attention economy's work. But, as I will argue, it is not the specific platform or medium that lies at the root of this eerie economy in which we are made to feed upon ourselves, turning desire and attention themselves into commodities we give away for free. Rather, it is the Interface: the complex and often invisible set of relations that conjoins individuality, longing, technology, and structural interests. Not all Interfaces are linked to screens, but all are linked to selves and their desires. Our self-commodification within the attention economy makes us unwitting labourers for capital. It also makes us serial sufferers of boredom, too often addicted to means that falsely promise alleviation and bring only repetition. Here we sit, shadow selves, hollowed out from within by alienation from our own attention.

These criticisms of the Interface and neoliberal boredom do not offer the standard-issue *Kulturkritik* reveal. Though I claim that some of the features of the Interface are invisible to us, and so require critical scrutiny, one of the most striking features of the attention economy is that it is ideological but not covert. Social media and online giants make no secret that they are gathering our data by playing on our desires to look, speak, and type. Only a surreptitious sale of data has the power to surprise – see Facebook and Cambridge Analytica – but even here the too-big-to-fail logic of Senate hearings, plus a large dose of old-guy internet incomprehension, carried the economic day.[2] It is, after all, surprising to those trained in Economics 101 that a multi-billion-dollar business could be sustained with no user fees. That's because the user fees are not paid in dollars, but in every user's time, psychic energy, and selfhood. We think we are using the tools of the Interface; in fact, the tools are using us. Boredom is the symptom here, not the disease. The metaphor is flawed but useful nonetheless: psychic restlessness is a virus in dormant condition; boredom is the disease become symptomatic; the engagements with the Interface mark the infectious stage. To vary metaphors from the clinical to mythical, we could also say that boredom is, crucially, the demon we wish to exorcise, the affliction we need to salve – and yet our usual methods for seeking relief do nothing except spread the inner blight of a soul at war with itself.

New economies create new workers, new commodities, and new injustices. The social costs of the attention economy have been documented: a rise in menial jobs like packaging Amazon products, which are then systematically phased out by automation, robotics, and drones; the dominance of short-term and service jobs that have no security and no infrastructure; the so far marginal but still significant costs of inactivity and screen-dominated life (obesity, illiteracy, etc.). But the central costs are perhaps less obvious. I will have more to say about the shifting relations of work and happiness in a later section; for now it is enough to notice that boredom is never just the property of imagination-poor teenagers or overimaginative philosophers. When we ourselves become the product we consume, the notion of work has decisively shifted. In the past, work was recognized for its colonizing power, expanding to fill and dominate time itself such that there might exist no clear line between work hours and non–work hours. Our current condition is worse. The Interface, leveraging boredom, makes us all into unpaid workers for the advertisers who support those apparently cost-free platforms. We ought to recall that there is no such thing as a free transaction. In this species of transaction, you pay with your individuality, freedom, and happiness.

WELLSPRING

According to a colleague of mine – I have not been able to confirm it independently – there was once to be seen in the Berlin U-Bahn system a poster depicting a young man with a dull expression on his face, the very image of a mind gone blank. The poster bore the legend, possibly ironic, *Die Langeweile ist der Ursprung des Philosophierens* (Boredom is the wellspring of philosophizing).

Langeweile has, of course, a longstanding tradition in German of indicating a state of boredom with particular significance; that is, not merely being enervated by a specific experience or person, but descending into a state of boredom we might legitimately call existential. The question remains, though, whether this state of being is properly associated with the origin of philosophical reflection, or what in phenomenology would be styled as a bracketing of the natural attitude in order to reveal the structure of consciousness itself. An alternative account of "origin" here would posit deep boredom as a necessary condition for reflection not just on the twinned burden and gift of consciousness, but also on the associated question of the meaning of life. Are we, when profoundly bored, especially susceptible to the large "philosophical" questions of mindedness, life, and death?

If one is to make such a claim, one must not merely defend boredom's status as a philosophy-inducing experience, but likewise compare it with other candidates for the origin-of-philosophy status. Traditionally these have included wonder (the Greek concept of *thaumazein*, as found in Plato's dialogues, especially *Theaetetus* and *Meno*[3]) and more direct confrontation with the prospect of death (as in Cicero's Socratically inflected claim that "to philosophize is to learn how to die"). Can boredom vie with these canonical, and apparently more respectable, accounts of the origin of the philosophical attitude? If so, what *kind* of boredom is in play? Is it distinct from what we might call "routine" or non-philosophical boredom? If so, how? Further, can the philosophy-inducing species of boredom be sought out actively, or does it visit us adventitiously? Are there specific mechanisms of reflection that leverage boredom into more active and explicit forms of philosophical thought?

But wait. What if the boredom that induces philosophical reflection is in fact coiled within, or inextricable from, the more familiar forms of philosophical prompting? Plato has Socrates relate the hoary tale of Thales of Miletus, astronomer and natural philosopher of vast gifts, who fell down a well as he walked along gazing at the wonders of the heavens. Was he moved to look up because of the dullness of mundane life around him? Thales found much to fascinate him in the ordinary world, but he was overwhelmingly fetched by the distant mysteries of the stars and the familiar feeling – an early antecedent to Kant's notion of the sublime – of our own insignificance in the universe around us. That feeling of sudden diminution of one's importance is not boredom as such but nevertheless feels close to it in the way that, as we shall see, procrastination and addiction are likewise cognate psychological states. Meaning drains from the scene, blotted out by the vastness of the real. We shrink to a tiny point, and routine thought – not to mention routine care about where I am walking – is obliterated. Wonder is usually considered uplifting, while boredom is thought enervating, but perhaps there is a closer affinity here than we usually imagine.

The point is confirmed by the learning-unto-death we find defended elsewhere in the Platonic corpus, the hard wisdom of our mortality shouldered not as a terrible burden but as a brave task. The optimistic version of this apparent death-cult tendency in Socratic thought is the Stoic acceptance of what cannot be otherwise, the embrace of the chilly but rational conclusion that death, like the time before birth, is simply a condition of non-being. Wittgenstein puts it this way: "Death is not an event in life; we do not live to experience death. If we take eternity to mean not infinite temporal duration but timelessness, then eternal life belongs to those who live in the present."[4] The "learning" relevant here is not meant in the usual sense of "how," as in "how-to," but rather in coming to view death with the proper perspective. Wittgenstein's emphasis on the temporal captures the affinity, perhaps unwilling, to boredom. Even as we might imagine immortality as "infinite temporal duration" – presumably a good thing – boredom teaches us that an intimation of this is all too common in daily life. What else is boredom, after all, than a feeling of time stretching out forever as an unbroken field: not the divine transcendence of the eternal present, Blake's "eternity in an hour," but a miserable series of drop-bottom moments that seems to go on forever without respite or rescue. That will teach you how to die, my friends, and do so such that the non-event of death, death as oblivion, might begin to seem positively attractive. This is the despair of boredom, which surely must put a person in a reflective mood about the looming emptiness of life, the fragility of our usual reasons for going on.

It is too facile, though, to flag boredom as philosophically in-teresting and then go about our mortal business as before. There is further investigation necessary here, which I hope to pursue with effect in the pages that follow. We must take seriously the idea that boredom is a philosophical wellspring, but also retain appropriate skepticism concerning the basic claims in favour of such philosoph-ical boredom. We must, in other words, attempt to reconstruct the phenomenology of any possible transition from the state of every-day boredom, almost always experienced as unpleasant or even hellish, to the (presumptively valuable) state of active philosophical reflection. The implications of this shift are obvious: if philosophical thought is indeed worth cultivating, then perhaps boredom has a special and heretofore underappreciated place in the range of every-day human consciousness.

But let caution rule our investigation. Perhaps the state of mind we call "reflection" is not, on further reflection, valuable after all.

This last turn of thought concerning thought might then open up the possibility that boredom serves not as a welcome, if unusual, invitation to insight, but rather as a kind of distant early warning system about the perils of consciousness becoming too aware of itself. Even as philosophy attempts to sort out the special status of boredom in its relations to desire, time (and the state, the discourse of philosophy – the sharp end of the stick doing the sorting) is liable to all kinds of threats that reduce itself to boring status. Philosophy's beginning is, in the peculiar fashion, also its end. This is what I propose to call the "Vicious Circle of Philosophical Boredom."

There is no escape from this circle, but I will suggest that there are more or less creative and happy ways in which we can approach our perpetual ensnarement in its always-renewing coils of consciousness.

WHY GO ON?

The psychoanalyst Adam Phillips begins one of his best essays this way: "Every adult remembers, among many things, the great ennui of childhood, and every child's life is punctuated by spells of boredom: that state of suspended anticipation in which things are started and nothing begins, the mood of diffuse restlessness which contains that most absurd and paradoxical wish, the wish for a desire."[5] The wish for a desire is a nod to Tolstoy's similarly doubled definition of boredom ("the desire for desires"). This twisted condition is not restricted to children, and though it may be judged absurd and paradoxical, it is nevertheless common and urgent. The stall of desire working against itself is the beginning, but not the end, of boredom. And thus boredom understood in terms of desire is a first clue to boredom's special ability to initiate philosophical reflection, but there are further clues to decipher and a more complicated solution to confront concerning the mystery of consciousness.

Schopenhauer is the dean of boredom studies, the first philosopher in the Western tradition to take seriously a condition that he recognized would become increasingly common. In part this was so because the material conditions of life allowed it: for a significant segment of the emergent bourgeois population, for whom the necessities of life were reliably secured, the questions of *what to desire* and *what to do* were no longer answerable in a straightforward, even pre-reflexive manner. As noted, the medieval philosophers and theologians had already dissected in some detail the particular vice of *accidie*, or melancholy torpor, which bears an emotional affinity to boredom. But this benighted condition, rooted alike in Greek and Christian notions of virtuous action, is shaded as a failure of spirit that might preclude the execution of one's duty, rather than an emotional and existential condition that is the wholly rational response to one's social and cultural condition.

Erich Fromm could, in the mid-twentieth century, note that what separates humans from other creatures is not the upright posture, or tool-wielding, or the ability to laugh, but rather precisely the fact that humankind is the only form of life blessed and cursed with the ability to query its own purpose. "Man is the only animal for whom his own existence is a problem which he has to solve and from which he cannot escape," Fromm wrote in *Man for Himself*, echoing earlier existential insight and confronting what he regarded as the "paralysis of our productive powers" that issues from the experience of boredom as an unavoidable part of that problem.[6] Boredom was, Fromm thought, an experience of everyday damnation. "I am convinced that boredom is one of the greatest tortures," he wrote. "If I were to imagine Hell, it would be the place where you were continually bored."[7]

All of this is prefigured in Schopenhauer's ground-breaking analysis, which anticipates by more than a century the sort of dissection of comfortable industrialized social existence that Fromm represents. Human life, says Schopenhauer in *The World as Will and Representation*, "swings like a pendulum to and fro between pain and boredom, and these two are in fact its ultimate constituents." Boredom is "anything but an evil to be thought of lightly: ultimately it depicts the countenance of real despair."[8] On one reading, a bored person is experiencing a species of psychic conflict, a *stall*. Seeking relief from pain, the organism moves toward stimulus. But since there is no particular desire to approve or make active as against any other, the self falls into a hopeless struggle with itself that cannot resolve, because there is no evident raw material on which to apply the energy of resolution. Boredom is, at its simplest, a form of desire turned back upon itself, resulting in the inability to act in any purposeful or happy manner. The hellishness of boredom, the real despair sketched on its countenance, is in large measure a function of the banality of the condition. Why can't I simply *want* something? Why can't I simply *do* something?

We are likely all too familiar with the experience: confronting the shelf of books where there is nothing to read; the enforced stillness of the long car journey with nothing to divert us from the unbroken vista out the window; the time spent waiting in queues, doctor's offices, or departure lounges; the long evenings that stretch out after one's lonely dinner without promise of incident or hint of pleasure. Boredom often, if not always, is experienced as a kind of temporal abyss, an acute awareness of time's passing; it is the existential variant of simple duration, deepening that mundane experience into an apparently endless waiting-for-nothing that suffuses and dominates consciousness.[9] In some ways, as we shall see, boredom acquires the character of an addiction, especially when it is actively cultivated by social conditions that can extract a profit from sustained bouts of boredom and stimulation. There is a danger that such an experience of boredom lowers the subject's resistance even as it raises the existential stakes. In contrast to the moments of quiet desperation described by classical authors, we might consider that the addict has it easy: even if he is powerless to solve it, at least he knows what his problem is!

I will presently separate some of these related strands concerning desire and temporality, since the experience of boredom – especially in relation to its ability to arouse philosophical reflection – is neither simple nor monolithic. Boredom does offer a profound opportunity for reflection on selfhood, indeed for philosophical investigation more generally. And there is ample room here for *irony*, a gift that may prove essential to the experience of philosophical boredom.

"People of experience maintain that it is very sensible to start from a principle," Kierkegaard writes in the *A* voice of *Either/Or*. "I grant them that and start with the principle that all men are boring."[10] The voice then goes on to offer a global theory of boredom that echoes Schopenhauer's lament from just fifteen years earlier:

> What wonder, then, that the world is regressing, that evil is gaining ground more and more, since boredom is on the increase and boredom is the root of all evil. We can trace this from the very beginning of the world. The gods were bored so they created man. Adam was bored because he was alone, so Eve was created. From that time boredom entered the world and grew in exact proportion to the growth of population. Adam was bored alone, then Adam and Eve were bored in union, then Adam and Eve and Cain and Abel were bored *en famille*, then the population increased and the people were bored *en masse*.[11]

Rarely has a comprehensive metaphysic been offered more briskly.

The *A* voice reflects further that, given there is no escape from this condition, there is no better strategy than the famous Kierkegaardian notion of "crop rotation": the application of arbitrary decisions, the "diverting" teasing of sensitive persons, and like divertissements. *A* makes a two-fold mistake here. First, he fails to see that, though there are indeed boring people, boredom may also be in the eye of the beholder. Everyone's mother likely admonished us, at some point, that only mentally impoverished or lazy people find themselves routinely bored. This the crux of Berryman's poem, quoted as an epigraph: confessing the condition of being bored is a self-indictment that one is, oneself, boring. This is not true, but it contains a germ of insight: sometimes the problem really is me, not you.

Second, though, and more seriously, *A* proposes to meet the condition of finding all people boring by substituting random or capricious desires for the desires, or interests, that they do not actually have. This, I suggest, is the essential error of accounts of boredom that conceive of it as primarily *dreadful*: that is, thinking that the solution to the stall of lacking a concrete desire is to find some – any – desire to fill the first-order void. But the desire so found or manufactured will inevitably have an arbitrary or bogus aspect, a taint of the very desperation it seeks to deny. Moreover, such trumped-up desires will always fail really to satisfy the background demands that desire and action be meaningful and so will fail to bring the happiness of psychic harmony. Instead, as experience often indicates, the restlessness of boredom is just continued by other means; we flit from desire to desire without being able to settle on any single one and endorse it as "resounding" (to use the language offered by Harry Frankfurt). Boredom is not to be defeated so easily.

Judge William's reply to *A*, in Kierkegaard's *Either/Or*, makes a version of this objection to over-simplistic defeat of boredom. He points out that only concrete ethical action will suffice to overcome the stall of boredom. In part this is a matter of Kierkegaard's longstanding antipathy to Hegelian dialectical idealism, which suggests that all conflicted states of mind, or spirit, are resolved into new *aufgehoben* syntheses. But it is also, or by the same token, a feature of Kierkegaard's notion of irony. Indeed, we find a complex insight about boredom in one of his earliest works, the dissertation he published *in propria persona* (as opposed to under one of his various pseudonyms) as *The Concept of Irony*. There we find this emphatic claim: "*Boredom* is the *only continuity* the ironist has. Yes, boredom: this eternity void of content, this bliss without enjoyment, this superficial profundity, this hungry satiety."[12] This may be construed as presaging the "root of all evil" passage in *Either/Or*, but I prefer to read it in a more active and positive manner. The ironist risks boredom, but it is, we might say, an active boredom, a militant irony. In contrast to the empty boredom of merely negative irony, this can yield action.[13]

Surely the task of going on living is the most overwhelming of them all? Why bother? And note that such despair can arise from too much fulfillment as easily as from too little. If life were a utopia where "pigeons flew about ready roasted," Schopenhauer wrote on the subject, invoking a standard image from the *Land of Cockaigne*, "people would die of boredom or else hang themselves."[14] The ironist answers that we are, in effect, already in the *Land of Cockaigne*, where almost any desire can be met and where, as a result, desire tangles itself in time-revealing knots of restless nothingness. The intriguing question is not whether this condition of mundane despair leads to a sad endgame of wanting to end both desire and time in the act of self-slaughter, as Hamlet called it.

Far more interesting is the apparently unreasonable fact that more people *do not* end their lives, that they go on enduring boredom even as it hollows out a sense of coherent self and meaningful relation of self to world. Surely this is a clue – albeit a dark and rather forbidding one – that boredom has much more to reveal to us than our own dread. Philosophy is born here, because *here* is the abyssal experience of everyday desire coming up against the question of meaning.

STALLED

Heidegger is the most distinguished of the many inheritors of the idea that philosophy issues from boredom in the form of anxiety. The central discussion occurs in the transcribed lectures from 1929–30 released in text form as *The Fundamental Concepts of Metaphysics: World, Finitude, Solitude.*[15] This course of lectures is justly famous for its expansive elaboration of Heidegger's nuanced thought about the deepest questions of philosophy in the period after *Being and Time* but before the later works of the post-war period. A key section, some hundred pages or more, is given over to boredom.

In this long – and, yes, sometimes boring – discussion, Heidegger enumerates three forms of boredom that mark the deepening sense of urgency brought about by the apparently routine experience. In much briefer terms than his, we can summarize the three forms this way: (1) boredom as extended waiting, a feeling that time stretches before us, brought on by some experience or feature of the world; (2) boredom of a generalized and slightly surprising sort, often noticed only post facto and not associated with a specific feature of the world, rather with a temporal range; and (3) what might be called

Orange County Airport
Southern California

Kodachrome by Harold Becraft

BETHLEHEM

Union Station, Bethlehem, Pa. — K-68-D-4

837   Waiting Room, Greyhound Bus Terminal, Pittsburgh, Pa.

2B-H1370

STOCK YARDS TRUCK STATION

45TH AND HALSTED   CHICAGO, ILLINOIS

BARNUM GARAGE & BARNUM AUTO RENTAL CORP.
508 Fairfield Ave., Bridgeport
Phone ED 5-2103

ONC-66—Tulsa Entrance to the Turner Turnpike, Tulsa, Oklahoma

TURNER TURNPIKE

3C-H952

Greetings from INDIANA TOLL ROAD

IMPERIAL '400' MOTEL
1221 E. 3rd St. • Winslow, Arizona

150—Medical Technician Barracks,
Fitzsimons General Hospital,
Denver, Colo.

fundamental boredom, boredom experienced as covering the entire expanse of Dasein's awareness of its own existence.

The first two forms are explored using specific examples that are among the most vivid in Heidegger's corpus. The boredom of waiting – the word cited here is of course *Langeweile* – is discussed with the mundane scenario in which one has missed or mistimed a train journey and must wait for a later train. There is in fact nothing to do but *wait*, and the waiting is experienced as a peculiar kind of burden, even (especially) as it is served out, we might say, in the specially designated Waiting Room of the railway station. "How do we escape this boredom [*Langeweile*], in which we find, as we ourselves say, that *time* becomes drawn out, becomes long [*lang*]?"[16] This rhetorical question contains a universe of everyday despair, for we do not escape it. Boredom of this sort is precisely what cannot be escaped! "This *profound boredom* is the *fundamental attunement*," Heidegger says. "We pass the time, in order to master it, because time becomes long in boredom. Time becomes long for us. Is it supposed to be short, then? Does not each of us wish for a truly long time for ourselves? And whenever it does become long for us, we pass the time and ward off its becoming long for us!"[17]

This paradox of long and short reveals why boredom matters. In being bored we are unsettled in our experience of the world. We are stalled in time, perhaps futilely blaming the railway station itself, and its implacable schedule, for exiling us in this manner. We are uncomfortable, wracked by a desire to be on our way – no matter how trivial the journey or the destination. "Profound boredom – a homesickness," Heidegger remarks. "Homesickness – philosophizing, we heard somewhere, is supposed to be a homesickness. Boredom – a fundamental attunement of philosophizing. *Boredom – what is it?*"[18] Now the question itself exhibits a certain desperation: what *is* it? As Heidegger immediately suggests, there is an "almost obvious" relation to time. This relation in turn reveals the three-fold question: world, finitude, and individuation. In order to see that question clearly, we need not only to resist the temptation to (as it were) chase boredom away but, more difficult still, avoid the tendency to identify boredom with what we imagine is its cause. This is the essence of Heidegger's key distinction between *boredom* and *boringness.*

Anything can be posited as the cause of boredom. This is part of its sustaining genius within the ambit of consciousness. Is it the train station itself that is boring? Or the play, or the dinner companion, or the stump speech? To imagine so is to make an error and so miss an opportunity. To use language somewhat divorced from Heidegger's existential-phenomenological discourse yet appositely related, let us ask, What is the perlocutionary force of the statement "I am bored"? On one level it is a self-reflective complaint: I am experiencing boredom right now. In addition, though, it sounds an implicit demand that the boredom *cease*, that the perceived cause of boredom (perhaps even one's current interlocutor or companion!) *stop being boring.*

But is this demand coherent, when anything at all might be seen (mistakenly?) as the cause of one's boredom? We might call this, after Stanley Cavell's notion of how apologies work, *transitive* boredom. That is, some boredom depends upon a complex relationship of the boring to the bored, and the boredom is structural to that relationship, not merely experienced as an isolated psychological condition. An example, drawn from the fiction of Kingsley Amis (himself a dedicated, if amateur, phenomenologist of boredom): "'From time to time,' said Graham weightily, 'my wife accuses me of thinking her boring. It doesn't seem to have occurred to her that this might be because she's boring.' Moving up to Patrick, he added man-to-man, 'To her mind, her being boring is a thing I do.'"[19] We are meant to sympathize with Graham's complaint, which is to say, to endorse the view (1) that there are objective standards of boringness, and (2) that his spouse has objectively violated them by being boring. Transitive boredom suggests a more complicated story: boredom is *at least* dyadic, a function of the bored encountering what he finds boring. But the middle term is, as so often, the most important yet least examined. In other words, how is it that something (anything, anyone) is *found to be* (experienced as) boring?

The contours of the dyad are variable with culture, and even language. A character in Edward St Aubyn's novel *Never Mind* notes that the English upper classes are especially boring in their desire *not* to be considered boring – "the terrible fear of being 'a bore,' and the boredom of the ways they relentlessly and narrowly evaded this fate."[20] Another character notes, "Only in the English language … can one be 'a bore,' like being a lawyer or a pastry-cook, making boredom into a profession – in other languages a person is simply boring, a temporary state of affairs." "What one aims for," another replies, "is ennui." Yet a third character, an American fed up with all this self-regarding British banter, pushes back: "Of course … [ennui] is more than just French for our old friend boredom. It's boredom plus money, or boredom plus arrogance. It's I-find-everything-boring, therefore I'm fascinating."[21]

Indeed: whatever the vagaries of English nouns, there is a reason that *this* form of boredom is denoted by an untranslatable French word; one cannot help think, here, of the line of *exquisitely* bored aesthetes who figure in the novels of Proust and Huysmans – also later to be celebrated by Oscar Wilde and Harold Acton, but gently mocked by Evelyn Waugh in the figure of Anthony Blanche, the stuttering dandy who languorously recites parts of Eliot's "The Waste Land" through a megaphone to a group of bemused undergraduates, and longs to get dunked in the college fountain by some *b-b-beefy b-b-boys* from the hearty athletic set. Charles Ryder, the first-person narrator of this odd tale of religious faith and alcoholism, is at first amused but eventually repulsed by Blanche's pose of drawling *Weltschmerzlich* superiority.

Perhaps this English, or more English than English, performance of "sophisticated" boredom is, in the end, merely boring? Or worse, perhaps it is a form of entrapment, fixing the other pole of the conversational dyad through the gravitational pull of endless talk and narcissism. The self-involved, however erudite, are like drunks: it's all about them. As a younger Amis, Kingsley's son Martin, would remark in a very different novel – *Night Train* – there is nobody more fatal than the barstool bore, the pissed philosopher. "Now he's swelling and swearing and sneering at the waitresses," the narrator says, a police detective observing a suspect in a hotel bar. "And boring the bartender blind: Asking the kid about his love life, his 'prowess', as if it's the feminine of *prow*. Jesus, aren't drunks a drag? Barmen know all about bores and boredom. It's their job. They can't walk away."[22]

In this story, we might note, the theme is precisely the kind of existential despair that might lethally visit not the sad but the happy. An unexplained death, an apparent suicide, has driven the narrator to this moment of observing someone who might be its cause. But the victim, beautiful and brilliant Jennifer Rockwell, would never have succumbed to the dubious charms of the boozy, second-rate Holiday Inn Lothario under surveillance, spreading his boringness like a virus or a bad smell. No, she committed her variation on self-slaughter for more metaphysical reasons, namely that there was just too little to expect even from a perfect life – looks, brains, career, blissful sex life with handsome philosopher boyfriend, and all. Mike Houlihan, the former homicide detective sent by Jennifer's agonized father, a police colonel, to find a murderer, can locate only ennui and emptiness.

Mike is a recovering alcoholic and she knows all about suicide. She knows the statistics about imitation, proximity, career suscept-ibility, inhibitors, and maybe above all the role that depressants can play. Alcoholism, she reflects, is "suicide on the installment plan" – a description applied earlier to F. Scott Fitzgerald, among others. Jennifer's death avoids the pay-as-you-go scheme of death by drug dependence, but her motives are not to be found in the standard psychological literature. What if, to shift the terms, bore-dom is murder on the instalment plan? What if our sublime cosmic insignificance overwhelms the tenuous bonds of life, even happy life? Then suicide might seem like the only way to stop the mun-dane torture, to limit the punishment of ordinary existence. Yes, and what if this mortal logic might convince the apparently con-tented as well as the aggrieved and downtrodden? Is it possible to be literally bored to death? Mike Houlihan, teasing out the threads of Jennifer's nihilistic decision, finds a string of false trails, blinds, and bleak jokes – the lies Jennifer left so that Mike, or someone, will have something to use in comfort for her grieving father. But this sense-making narrative is bogus, and Mike knows it. "What else can I tell him?" Mike bleakly wonders near the novel's end. "Sir, your daughter didn't have motives. She just had standards. High ones. Which we didn't meet."[23]

High terms of meaning and significance, which the indifferent universe mocks. And so a recovering alcoholic like Mike might be driven by this dreadful sequence of events back into the false comforts of drink – the cause of, and solution to, all of life's problems.[24] And thus do the bored become the boring, through immersion in whisky. It is also, in Mike's case as in so many others, how the quick become the dead.

WHAT DOES IT ALL MEAN?

Heidegger's second and third forms of boredom pursue this cluster of questions insistently, never content to offer the lazy self-congratulation of aristocratic (or maybe faux-aristocratic, hipsterized) ennui. The central example in the first form was the obviously boring experience of "dead time" at a train station: "How much time is capable of here! It has power over railway stations which can bring it about that stations bore us."[25] But the second form is even more intriguing. "We have been invited out somewhere for the evening … So we go along. There we find the usual food and the usual table conversation, everything is not only very tasty, but very tasteful as well… There is nothing at all to be found that might have been boring about this evening, neither the conversation, nor the people, nor the rooms. Thus we come home quite satisfied… [A]nd then it comes: I was bored after all this evening, on the occasion of this invitation."[26] *Yet how so?* Heidegger immediately wants to know. And yet, of course the answer is all too obvious: if the first form of boredom was an experience mainly of *frustration* over time dragging, this form is an indication of ennui concerning the meaninglessness of time even when pleasantly spent. In short, when it comes to time, spending is all too often just wasting; and now the lack of frustration, precisely the smoothness of time so wasted, acts as a sort of prophylactic against the generalized infection of boredom.

Thus this "more profound" form of boredom, though perhaps inoperative in itself, in part because nothing in particular is here found boring, pushes us inexorably to the confrontation with time that has been lurking all along. Chatting our lives away "in a casual manner," as Heidegger puts it, must eventually force the issue: *boredom springs from the temporality of Dasein*. If form-one boredom seemed to come, as it were, from outside, form-two boredom is clearly a matter of Dasein's own inner summons.

Enter the third form of boredom, and the only one properly effective in arousing a truly philosophical attitude. Here Heidegger – ironically, "following our vacation" in the academic term – identifies the comprehensive boredom proper to philosophy. It is, he says, associated with no example or experience; rather, it is captured by the general phrase "It is boring for one."[27] It is boring for one to walk through the city. It is boring for one to spend the afternoon reading. It is boring for one to plan and execute a family dinner. It is boring for one *to be here at all*. Self-evidently, there is no "cure" or alternative to this boredom, no way its reach can be outrun or its wiles outwitted. Now, perhaps for the first time, frustration and ennui give way to a kind of despair. "When a man is tired of London," Dr Johnson famously said, "he is tired of life." Precisely – because there is no end to the objective stimulations of that great city. More precisely, the end of stimulation is a sign of a profound malaise with temporal existence itself. This "emptiness," Heidegger notes, "makes *everything of equally great and equally little worth*."[28] Once value is so deflated, life itself is worthless.

The good news, of course, is that for Heidegger "this 'it is boring for one' – from whatever depths it may arise – does not have the character of despair."[29] The impersonal "one" (rather than "me") indicates an originary condition, not an affliction but a basic feature of the Dasein operating system. Now "we can *give the word boredom, 'Langeweile,' a more essential meaning*." That is, "In boredom, and indeed especially in this form when 'one is bored,' this while of Dasein becomes long … The lengthening of the while is the *expansion of the temporal horizon*, whose expansion does not bring Dasein liberation or unburden it, but precisely the converse in *oppressing* with its expanse."[30] One might think that Heidegger's "boredom is oppressive but not desperate" rivals the wry Viennese saying that "the situation is desperate but not serious," without the latter's liberating irony. But though there is indeed no liberation here, there is new wisdom. In sum, and as usual with italics in the original, *boredom impels entranced Dasein into the moment of vision as the properly authentic possibility of its existence.*"[31] Boredom, in its generalized indifference to the world, urgently raises the basic questions of philosophy. "These are not merely bookish or literary questions, nor questions that belong to some movement or school of philosophy, but rather questions posed by the essential need of Dasein itself."[32]

In a final flourish, Heidegger neatly defeats those who imagine that philosophy, in the sense of erudition and "reading and reviewing philosophical literature," is the answer to this same question: this, too, is an attempt at overcoming or unburdening. "Only if we experience its essence from out of philosophizing itself will we become intimate with the essence of philosophy … Philosophy is only there to be overcome." There is, indeed, a kind of letting go that is here enjoined: "This profound boredom only becomes awake if we do not counteract it."[33]

Thus the fundamental questions of philosophy arise in boredom, not uniquely perhaps but insistently. What is a world? What is individuation? What is finitude? The "bland triviality" of missing a train or enduring a pleasant but mundane dinner party reveal the deep heart of existence, the "abyssal difficulty of the problem" of being here in the first place, of being at all.

TEST-BED OF POLITICAL IMAGINATION

It is perhaps to be expected that Adorno would grow impatient with the lack of structural specificity in any universal existential account of boredom. In the exquisitely cranky late essay "Free Time," which includes the guts of Adorno's own account of boredom, Heidegger goes unmentioned; instead, Adorno excoriates Schopenhauer, the longer-standing and more accessible philosophical relative, for the blind spot of assuming that a particular condition of work/leisure tension should be construed as basic to the human predicament.[34] "At an early age Schopenhauer formulated a theory of boredom," he notes. "True to his metaphysical pessimism he teaches that people either suffer from the unfulfilled desires of their blind will, or become bored as soon as these desires are satisfied."[35]

Schopenhauer was just twenty-six years old when he formulated his theory of will and representation, something Nietzsche (himself no slouch in the early-genius sweepstakes) found significant, since it suggests an upsweeping of desire that, sublimated into philosophical neurosis, inspired a predictable self-protective gesture in the form of asceticism. Adorno does not psychologize after this fashion. Instead, he notes that basic problem of taking one's own state as indicative of a universal condition. "One should not hypostatize Schopenhauer's doctrine as something of universal validity," Adorno argues, "or even as an insight into the primal character of the human species." Instead, applying more concrete categories of cultural materialism, we should see that "boredom is a function of life which is lived under the compulsion to work, and under the strict division of labour. It need not be so."[36]

Both the diagnosis and the suggestion of alternative structural arrangement are typical. Indeed, "Free Time" is a brief and effective distillation of all that is idiosyncratic and enjoyable in Adorno's cultural criticism. The basic claim of the essay is familiar enough: under late-capitalist conditions, the force of the work idea is such that even the hours outside of work are colonized by the imperatives of use, assimilation, and the constant reproduction of consumption cycles. So-called free time – the time of the weekend or after the whistle blows, the time of TGIF and leisure – is not free at all. Unlike the genuine leisure of the Greek ideal, where *skhole* (σχολή) functions as time free of all concern except contemplation of ultimate realities, it is preconditioned and desperate. "Free time is shackled to its opposite," Adorno says. "Indeed the oppositional relation in which it stands imbues free time with certain essential characteristics."[37] These characteristics include the false idea that free time is recreational in some deep or authentic sense, rather than being, in effect, a battery-recharging station for the vast matrix of work itself. Free time, Adorno continues in the same passage, "depends on the totality of social conditions, which continues to hold people under its spell."

And so the appearance that free time is a contrast, even perhaps a subversive challenge, to the hegemony of time organized by work is shattered: the opposite is in fact the case; the two are allies, twinned sides of the same ideological coin. "Free time then does not merely stand in opposition to labour. In a system where full employment itself has become the ideal, free time is nothing more than a shadowy continuation of labour."[38] This is dire, but there is hope for challenge in the emerging contours of this internal contradiction. Free time – Adorno encloses the phrase in ironic quotation marks, what we would now call "scare quotes" – "is tending toward its own opposite, and is becoming a parody of itself. Thus unfreedom is gradually annexing 'free time,' and the majority of unfree people are as unaware of this process as they are of the unfreedom itself."[39] Once this is perceived, presumably the stranglehold of free time, acting as a hidden agent of the work world, will be broken.

At once, and again perhaps typically, Adorno dashes his own theoretical hope. In part this is a matter of his own ingrained intellectual elitism. Many people, he notes, claim to enjoy "hobbies" in their free time, and these "hobbies" – one imagines here a basement workshop for woodworking gear, or sheds full of golf clubs and fishing rods – simply distract one from the unfreedom of free time. Thus one of the most theory-laden definitions of "hobby" that one is ever likely to run across: "the expression 'hobby' amounts to a paradox: that human condition which sees itself as the opposite of reification, the oasis of unmediated life within a completely mediated total system, has itself been reified just like the rigid distinction between labour and free time."[40] Adorno, by contrast, spends his time reading, writing, and listening to music. These are not hobbies, they are intellectual activities.

In sum, the message is something like this: "I am Teddie Adorno, and *you're not*. You have hobbies, I have intellectual pastimes of a higher order of seriousness. So there!" Naturally this is a false move of considerable proportion, inviting as it does the sort of response that Pierre Bourdieu would deliver against all such self-forgiving value-judgments within the exercise of taste.[41] There is no blind spot more expansive and opaque than the one deployed by intellectuals who think their own taste-driven distinctions are inherently valid when all others are not. In short, one person's hobbies cannot trump another's when it comes to worthiness, even – indeed especially – on Adorno's own account of unfree "free time."

I won't pursue that objection here, except to note that Adorno's self-approval colours the subsequent judgments about how people spend their non-work hours, which brings us finally to his account of boredom, which has merit, even accepting the shaky state of the path that gets us to it. After dismissing hobbies in general, Adorno is particularly withering about two pastimes that seem to rouse in him an extra degree of ire: camping and sunbathing. The former, very popular with European youngsters at the time of the essay's composition, is denounced in terms that can be likewise found in other contemporary sources, such as the nascent Situationist movement, but also in less obviously theoretical places such as older conservation movements that found postwar camping vogues to be jejune and superficial. Modern camping, the charge goes, is a bogus form of chasing after authenticity. In the guise of a "return to nature" it is in fact merely an adjunct to the usual rounds of production and consumption, especially in the form of what we might call gear-porn. Camping invents the natural world in something like the same fashion that Turner's paintings invent the sunset: the natural world commodified and framed for easy ingestion.

This is familiar territory, as I say, and the main interest now might simply be that there is considerable push-back in recent thinking about camping (see, for example, Matthew de Abaitua's study of the subject[42]). The case against sunbathing is, if anything, more bizarre. Adorno views this abomination of free time as a clear illustration of Hegel's notion of the abstract or vacuous condition of apparently advanced consciousness. The basic indictment is worth quoting at fair length: "An archetypal instance is the behaviour of those who grill themselves brown in the sun merely for the sake of a sun-tan, although dozing in the blazing sunshine is not at all enjoyable, might very possibly be physically unpleasant, and certainly impoverishes the mind." This last point is never validated or even adequately explained; Adorno hurries on. "In the sun-tan, which can be quite fetching, the fetish character of the commodity lays claim to actual people; they themselves become fetishes. The idea that a girl is more erotically attractive because of her brown skin is probably only another rationalization. The sun-tan is an end in itself, of more importance than the boy-friend it was perhaps supposed to entice."[43]

One may dispute the details here, not to mention the passage's own unquestioned ideological assumptions, especially about gender roles; but it is here that the fortress of modern boredom must be breached. "The act of dozing in the sun marks the culmination of a crucial element of free time under present conditions – boredom."[44] People are so bored in their free time that, on occasion, they do not even recognize the fact. In the sometimes frenetic pursuit of pleasure in weekend activities we can observe flights from awareness that both Adorno and Heidegger would recognize. In calmer pursuits such as camping, quiet hobbies, and seemingly purpose-free time-wasting such as sunbathing, the rush to escape is just as basic but covered by a blanket of semi-conscious political assumptions about the contrast – in fact a complicity – between work and free time. Adorno's important contribution here is to see that the tangles of desire are a function not of hard-wired human psychology, or even of one's primordial relation to temporality, but of specific *and therefore changeable* social conditions. As so often in the work of the Frankfurt school's brand of *Kulturkritik*, the bottom line is a call for emancipation. Or, to be more precise, self-emancipation. Adorno can do only so much in the way of acerbic commentary on the doltish tendencies of modern life. The sunbathers must rouse themselves and cast off the chains of their tanning lotions and cocoa-butter unguents! That commercial tanning bed, meanwhile, is merely the grave of political consciousness!

This is all very well, after its fashion, but we are confronted with a familiar dilemma, or endgame. The "seeing-through" moment of critical-theoretic reflection on aspects of everyday life does not seem, of itself, to make emancipation any more likely. Nor, indeed, are we always convinced that emancipation is the correct program of response to even a highly critical awareness of those everyday activities. Sometimes perhaps it is enough simply to stop tanning. Granting these caveats, it is nevertheless invigorating to see in Adorno a philosophical but also political direction emerging from the experience of boredom. Boredom is political, because it illustrates the simultaneous emptiness and non-autonomous nature of our existence. "If people were able to make their own decisions about themselves and their lives, if they were not caught up in the realm of the eversame, they would not have to be bored," Adorno says. "Boredom is the reflection of objective dullness. As such it is in a similar position to political apathy."[45]

The most pernicious feature of boredom might be, finally, that it makes us forget that boredom is political in this fashion. It is, in a low hum of not-thinking and not-desiring, an especially toxic form of false consciousness afflicting people living under the yoke of "free time." "Failing to discern the relevance of politics to their own interests, they retreat from all political activity," Adorno concludes. "The well-founded or indeed neurotic feeling of powerlessness is intimately bound up with boredom: boredom is objective desperation. It is also, however, symptomatic of the deformations perpetrated upon man by the social totality, the most important of which is surely the defamation and atrophy of the imagination."[46]

To which the most measured response might be: *important if true*. The open question here, one foreclosed by Adorno's own assumptions about the neurotic emptiness of people's minds during boredom, is whether imagination is indeed deformed by being bored. I will argue that it is not, though once more Adorno's contribution to the relation of boredom to philosophy is not thereby negated. On the contrary, we can see in boredom's own groping self-awareness not a prison where consciousness is trapped in self-cancelling vacuity, but instead a possible test bed of just those possibilities of political imagination about which Adorno is worried. Once more, but now with a new political inflection, boredom is not the end but the beginning.

LEARNING TO WAIT

In a curious but not unprecedented fashion, contemporary psychology and neuroscience appear to confirm the more literary insights of an earlier century of philosophical reflection. "Boredom is, paradoxically, a motivating force/catalyst for action," a 2014 study argues. "Boredom might stimulate the need to redecorate, take up a new hobby, or look for a new job. The feeling, then, can induce challenge-seeking behavior, and therein lies the paradox that boredom, associated by many with lethargy, can actually be energizing, inspiring a search for 'change and variety.'"[47]

To be sure, these recent advocates of *creative boredom* take the motivating aspects of boredom – boredom seen as the origin of a reflective, perhaps philosophical attitude – as little more than a spur to overcoming the supposed "lethargy" of the condition. The central conclusion here is the following: evidence "suggests that boredom can sometimes be a force for good. This means that it might be a worthwhile enterprise to allow or even embrace boredom in work, education, and leisure. On an individual basis, if one is trying to solve a problem or come up with creative solutions, the findings from our studies suggest that undertaking a boring task (especially a reading task) might help with coming up with a more creative outcome."[48] When we examine the psychological literature more closely, what is revealed is a therapeutic program to redeem boredom by repositioning its presumptively negative features as opportunities for creative thought, and thus not unlike daydreaming, wool-gathering, brainstorming, and other "outside the box" or "lateral thinking" tactics. Construed as *tactical*, indeed, this therapeutic taming or domestication of boredom evades what truly philosophical boredom promises: not future relief, but renewed anxiety. So-called creative boredom takes boredom only half-seriously, avoiding the Vicious Circle of Boredom – the self-renewing and ever-deepening cycles of the boredom experience – by an anxious recast. Never fear! Boredom may seem disagreeable, but in fact it contains a kernel of creative possibility!

This is profoundly wrong, not least because it attempts an end-run on the truly boring experience of encountering one's own boredom. Philosophical boredom is not less boring for being philosophical; on the contrary. Heidegger understands this: boredom is the origin of philosophy because of the questions it forces upon us; but the beginning is also the end, because the principled investigation of boredom brings no relief. It is very much like the general paradox observable in philosophical attempts to apprehend the notion of common sense: the more we investigate this most proximate of categories, the more uncommon our understanding becomes. The philosopher faces the peculiar dilemma of seeing, perhaps more clearly than anyone else, that the world one encounters must remain *exactly as it is*, if it is to be known at all, even as she or he knows, in a somewhat bowel-shrivelling fashion, that letting things alone is just what philosophical investigation cannot do.

Worse still, perhaps, is the creeping awareness that our attempts to apprehend the world, and our experience of it, may have to embrace boredom in order to appreciate nuance more fully. The eminent analytic philosopher Timothy Williamson articulates the stakes very well here. "Impatience with the long haul of technical reflection is a form of shallowness, often thinly disguised by histrionic advocacy of depth," he writes in a heavy volume titled *The Philosophy of Philosophy*.[49] And so, "Serious philosophy is always likely to bore those with short attention-spans." Nor is this immanent imperative restricted to the Heideggers of the philosophical world. "Much even of analytic philosophy moves too fast in its haste to reach the sexy bits," Williamson avers. "Details are not given the care they deserve: crucial claims are vaguely stated, significantly different formulations are treated as though they were equivalent, examples are under-described, arguments are gestured at rather than properly made, their form is left unexplained, and so on."

One may legitimately wonder what the "sexy bits" are in the discourse of analytic philosophy, widely noted for its reader-repelling dryness and technicality, but the general stakes are recognizable across all styles of philosophical engagement. "Shoddy work is sometimes masked by pretentiousness, allusiveness, gnomic concision, or winning informality. But often there is no special disguise: producers and consumers have simply not taken enough trouble to check the details." This quandary calls for a special kind of response, in Williamson's view: "We need the unglamorous virtue of patience to read and write philosophy that is structured as perspicuously as the difficulty of the subject requires, and the austerity to be dissatisfied with appealing prose that does not meet those standards." In sum: "The fear of boring oneself or one's readers is a great enemy of truth." (One review of this ponderous book commented that that particular fear is one "which Williamson ruthlessly masters."[50])

One is tempted to respond that this conclusion itself is too quick, and too slick – a sexy bit of paradox, arguing in favour of two-fold boredom in philosophy. The conclusion seems, at the least, a potential escape hatch: why bother to expend energy in explaining the appeal, value, or urgency of philosophical questions when one has the iron-clad presumptive defence that the matter is *supposed* to be boring. But no, not so fast. Philosophical reflections about boredom, and boredom as the origin of philosophy, up the ante here *and* clarify the Issues. Philosophy is supposed to be hard, but that does not necessitate its being boring. There is, in other words, a yet more advanced view concerning the Vicious Circle of Boredom, one that transcends Williamson's virtue of boring patience without obviating its limited value within particular debates.

The key here, I think, is to surrender the impulse, shared by so-called creative and some philosophical accounts, to turn boredom itself into a virtue. Boredom is unpleasant, enervating, frustrating, and sometimes even immiserating. We should not imagine that a positive outcome arising from this experience – new creative ideas or philosophical insights – rehabilitates the original experience. Indeed, it is only because boredom is *enduringly unpleasant* that it has the potential to play a role in arousing the philosophical attitude: we cannot move to a questioning of how meaning is possible in the world unless we have really experienced the awful reality of a (temporary) condition in which there is no meaning. The lived reality of meaninglessness is, we might say, a necessary condition of the investigation of meaning's possibility. To think otherwise is merely to succumb to a more sophisticated version of the routine evasions of boredom evident in such things as the desperately lively social round, immersion in distracting media, and a relentless general commitment to any and all activities that drive away the chance of doing and thinking nothing in particular – as, perhaps, when we are stuck on a long U-Bahn journey.

We must learn, in other words, to wait, cultivating the kind of *savoir-attendre* posture that Guy Debord, for example, advocates towards the end of *The Society of the Spectacle*: "Thus madness reappears in the very posture which pretends to fight it. Conversely, the critique which goes beyond the spectacle must *know how to wait*" (Par là le délire s'est reconstitué dans la position même qui prétend le combattre. Au contraire, la critique qui va au-delà du spectacle doit *savoir attendre*).[51] Blithe critique of the spectacle merely reconstitutes its errors in a new, delirious form; instead, it is necessary that effective critique possess a kind of quiet patience – not to be confused with Williamson's stepwise technical drudgery.

Likewise, and frequently on the same cultural and political ground, the primary wisdom of boredom is not to be found in the philosophical insights to which it might give rise, important though these may be. The value is, rather, in the very openness to such waiting that alone allows boredom to flourish. "Against boredom even the gods themselves struggle in vain," Nietzsche said in *The Antichrist*.[52]

Just so. The gods cannot save us here. We can only save ourselves – not by contending with boredom in the hope of defeating it or fighting it off, finally, but rather by welcoming, albeit with some dread, its slow, insistent, energy-draining call. Then, and only then, are we in a position to philosophize. If we are lucky, *pace* Williamson, the results thus produced will not themselves be boring; but there are no guarantees, and being bored by philosophical discourse may be, ironically, one of the central wellsprings of the genuine philosophical attitude. That, at least, has been the experience of generations of students stuck in airless lecture halls, wondering why they are there …

CATEGORIES

We might now, on the basis of this preliminary taxonomy, articulate the following distinct categories of boredom, or of boredom's etiology and function. This categorization of boredom will prove necessary in any attempt to advance the boredom discourse further, or, more accurately, to return it to what I view as its proper place as political problem. That is to say, I want to isolate the special contemporary case of neoliberal boredom, and then pursue the question of how that form of boredom links intricately with contemporary conditions of selfhood and unhappiness. Other forms of boredom, especially the so-called *creative* mode of the condition, will remain relevant throughout subsequent investigation. To be sure, the following conceptual categories are not as fixed or impermeable as strict philosophical analysis would prefer. They also, as usual, have the effect, as categories, of retroactively finding evidence that fits the attendant conceptual scheme. Nevertheless, because neoliberal boredom is an ideological formation as well as a conceptual one, and a formation therefore with tendencies to invisibility in its deep effects if not its prima facie presence, it is worthwhile to tease apart these threads in the general fabric of boredom before we go on. It seems to me there are five distinct forms or modalities of boredom that can be distinguished.

1 Boredom as Philosophically Originary

The investigation so far has been focused on this category or understanding of boredom. I will therefore summarize only briefly before offering more detail on the subsequent four categories of boredom I wish to distinguish. The standard philosophical accounts of boredom bear a common air of mild self-congratulation under their various differences of emphasis. Schopenhauer, Kierkegaard, and Heidegger are the prominent figures here, as we know, each suggesting that the subjectively unpleasant experience of boredom is philosophically revelatory. Put crudely, the notion is that the experience of finding oneself bored induces an existential crisis of dimensions serious enough to throw one's easygoing selfhood into question. Why are my desires so tangled that I cannot frame a single coherent one, instead lurching from impasse to impasse? It has been said with some justice that boredom is a condition that emerges only with modernity, with its opportunities for aimless desire and time without explicit purpose. We could go further: boredom may be the essential feature of the modern condition, since it marks the state of the self as confused concerning its own routes to satisfaction.

It is worth emphasizing that not only does this conception of boredom mark the condition as philosophically originary, but also that, in a neat symmetry, this philosophical conception is the originary account of boredom. That is, these philosophers' understanding of boredom as a crisis of selfhood and desire that must be embraced is what we ought to regard as the *standard view* of boredom, against which other (especially more contemporary) notions are advanced. This is significant for present purposes because a return to philosophical boredom – as distinct from the notions of boredom that seek to nullify it or deflect it – is part of the critical argument I am advancing. I will also add a political dimension to this return, based in part on Adorno's account of boredom (see below), but with contemporary twists.

2 Psychoanalytic Boredom

As in Kierkegaard, the closest cousin in the traditional philosophical discourse on boredom, the focus here is on what we might call "tangles of desire" – when desires conflict or do not align between first and second orders, when specific desire is numbingly absent, and so on. Of all possible accounts of boredom, the ones centred on analysis of desire, especially desire tangled, come closest to the true stakes of this everyday experience. Too often lacking, however, are the social and structural dimensions of the tangles, especially in relation to capital and technological conditions of the day.

Phillips's "wish for a desire" highlights a genuine paradox, unlike the merely instrumental one of creative boredom. The stall of desire acting against itself is the beginning, not the end, of boredom. And thus boredom illuminates desire, consciousness, and the thrust for meaning. Here we are blocked, our longings thwarted by their own gear-grinding mechanisms; or, to vary the mechanical metaphor, the clutch is unconsciously in and the throttle is being revved to maximum. There is no possible traction because the engine is not properly engaged. To quote Eliot, who understood at least part of the problem, we are "Distracted from distraction by distraction. / Filled with fancies and empty meaning. / Tumid apathy with no concentration."[53] Desire becomes a sort of mad master or deranged parent, constantly insisting upon attention without allowing clear paths to its deployment. And so double-binds are set in place, where all actions are losing moves that only tighten the tangle, like a knot in a mass of dropped fishing line.

In traditional psychoanalytic terms, it may be said that, in the case of boredom, unconscious desires are being suppressed not in the form of, or displaying the symptoms of, neurosis; rather, the general paralysis of desire is a comprehensive neurotic manifestation of blockage. Hence the restlessness and indistinct dissatisfaction of boredom: I am vaguely annoyed at my own inability to form a coherent desire, and yet not sufficiently so to break out of the paralytic condition. So many channels, and nothing on! Thus Phillips will argue that boredom acts as a sort of psychic prophylactic under conditions of confusion and haphazard desire. "Boredom, I think, protects the individual, makes tolerable for him the impossible experience of waiting for something without knowing what it could be," he writes. "So that the paradox of the waiting that goes on in boredom is that the individual does not know what he was waiting for until he finds it, and that often he does not know that he is waiting."[54] This in turn echoes the judgment of historian of boredom Peter Toohey, that "boredom is, in the Darwinian sense, an adaptive emotion. Its purpose, that is, may be designed to help one flourish."[55] It is significant that

Toohey, a classical scholar, chooses the verb "flourish" here, which cannot help having Aristotelian overtones of virtue and the deep-seated form of happiness – "living and faring well," as the ancient philosopher put it – called *eudaimonia*. But now we may be shading over into what is usually called "creative" boredom (see section 4 below), or back into philosophical boredom (1).

Phillips says in the same essay that boredom is "akin to free-floating attention," which might likewise suggest the sort of productive wool-gathering associated with creative boredom. "Boredom," he argues, "is integral to the process of taking one's time." When our attention floats free, especially as the result of a psychic blockage or stall, perhaps new happiness options will open up, new breakthroughs become possible. Perhaps. But "free-floating" is an unstable condition, such that the free-floating signifier in semiotics, for example, creates only confusion and disarray. Words like *freedom* and *justice*, say, are so open-ended in their possible referents as to become entirely detached from agreed-upon sense, an example of what Jennifer Egan calls "word-casings": sloughed-off carapaces or husks left over when living organisms or genuine referents have departed the semantic scene when they have been shucked of sense.[56] Under such conditions, where attention and language are alike free-floating, meaning has no meaning, and desire no fixed object – not even one "retroactively posited," as Lacan and Žižek insist is the case.[57] Cathexis is, on their account, pervasive and undifferentiated as such, seeking organization but lacking it in the absence of structures of meaning. Objects of desire are therefore not already present in the world before we enter it, as most of us assume, so much as they are created by our need to want something in particular, to *fixate*. And this fixation in turn is part of the retroactive positing of selfhood.

We will see, in part 2 of this book, that *truth* is now one such word-casing, contributing to the complications of what I am here calling "The Condition." As I argued in earlier work, the notion of word-casings raises the spectre of even more comprehensive effects. Are we now, in effect, *person-casings*, mere leftover shells of the more robust individuals we once thought, and still sometimes imagine, ourselves to be?[58] The person-casing is not in a condition of desire denied; instead it experiences the world as made up of too many desires, so multifarious that they cancel each other out in a buzz of noise over signal, so that even retroactive positing of selfhood becomes a mug's game, a self-administered con. This low-level infernal imprisonment within the labyrinths of promised but illusory individuation would, then, be another way to describe the zombification of the self under current political and technological conditions. And once again, boredom is a key locus of our critical attention – if we can exert the effort to put ourselves into question.

3 Political Boredom

Adorno's delineation of the dangers of "leisure" or "free time" under capitalism is the core text here. On this view, there is not nearly enough emphasis in the current discourses devoted to boredom and technology on the specifically political dimensions of the subject. Even where Adorno's account is considered, for example – television and leisure time – there is little attempt to update critical considerations for the peculiar and unprecedented conditions of our world. People do not watch television in the way they used to, after all, nor is leisure time confined to evenings and weekends understood as distinct from (and so an unwitting enabler of) work-time. Any critique of the current state of subjectivity and its relations to media must take full account of the urgency of the issue – not with further hand-wringing or laying of blame, but with nuanced structural analysis. Boredom is not simply a mildly irritating everyday experience, nor is it an existential condition beyond further investigation; it is, in its own peculiar way, a call to arms.

Adorno's critique of political boredom is deeply bound up with a general critique of the elisions operating between the notions of work and leisure. Leisure time is either co-opted to work time in the form of "playful" elements in the workplace – slides, fun rooms, casual dress codes, pet accommodation, etc. – or leisure time is itself made into a site of exertion and competition. Sometimes the two forms operate at once. Thus the frenzied rounds of weekend fun so typical of the modern worker, which bespeak a profound inability to break out of the general bonds of work. Thus the boredom of contemporary leisure time is a function of a more profound enervation, what descends when one is reduced to one's work-self. Boredom is political, under this analysis, because it signals a sense that all is not well in the arrangements of labour and selfhood, and individuals hopelessly suspended in the nets of what I have elsewhere called "the work idea." The work idea is not paid work as such, still less the noble labour one might imagine is possible within a sense of vocation, but the pervasive and mostly unchallenged idea that one must work in order to be present in the world at all. Adorno's analysis, still relevant, needs updating, however. The erosion of central work sites and the emergence of a widespread "gig economy," where workers desperately piece together a scant livelihood out of short-term and often unregulated jobs, signals a new form of capitalist exploitation and marginalization.

Gig workers are not alienated from their labour in the traditional sense of having labour's products commodified and sold for a profit in which they do not share. Rather, the gig economy produces a deeper and more pernicious form of alienation, that of the worker from himself or herself, stuck in a job whose very existence is structured by the whims of others. At the same time, the general imperatives of work, that it fosters engagement and self-reliance, are ratcheted constantly to suggest that one can never work hard enough. "Inspirational" tales abound of gig workers going the extra mile, such as the pregnant Lyft driver who insisted on delivering her passenger even as she went into labour. "It does require a fairly dystopian strain of doublethink for a company to celebrate how hard and how constantly its employees must work to make a living, given that these companies are themselves setting the terms," the critic Jia Tolentino wrote. "And yet this type of faux-inspirational tale has been appearing more lately, both in corporate advertising and in the news."[59]

The gig-site Fiverr, for example, which touts itself eponymously as "an online marketplace for freelance services" where some offerings sell for as little as five dollars, ran an ad campaign in 2017 called "In Doers We Trust." As the press-release copy had it, "The campaign positions Fiverr to seize today's emerging zeitgeist of entrepreneurial flexibility, rapid experimentation, and doing more with less. It pushes against bureaucratic overthinking, analysis-paralysis, and excessive whiteboarding." Which sounds … well, it sounds incomprehensible, though gesturing at something "revolutionary" to cut through boring middle-management bureaucracy. As Tolentino remarks, however, "This is the jargon through which the essentially cannibalistic nature of the gig economy is dressed up as an aesthetic." Critical analysis of why gigging is necessary in the first place is not over-thinking; blithely accepting this as the new economic reality is, if anything, unforgivable under-thinking.

The gig worker's boredom, always uncertain, always waiting for another gig, is therefore distinct from the boredom of the line cook, cubicle drone, or factory-floor toiler. The "hurry-up-and-wait" of gigging connects strongly with other locations of that dispiriting imperative: the grinding boredom of foot soldiers, say, by whom the phrase was probably invented. One can counter this boredom by accepting the cheerful "doer" ethos of the Fiverr campaign, but let it be said that this is a form of insanity. These workers are like the crazed marathon dancers in *They Shoot Horses, Don't They?* (1969), that bleak parable of Depression-era desperation – the boredom of ceaseless striving in a rigged competition.

Not that matters are much better in more stable forms of work. Those working in what David Graeber brusquely calls "bullshit jobs" – occupations that create no meaning or value – are similarly ensnared by the capitalist illusion that work, while boring, is somehow necessary.[60] Graeber, who has also written vividly about the debt cycles structurally embedded in capitalist systems, attacks a range of mostly white-collar jobs that are useless and known by their occupants to be so: human-resources consultants, communication coordinators, telemarketing researchers, corporate lawyers. He affixes labels to various categories of bullshit job (Goons, Flunkies, Box Tickers, Duct Tapers, and Taskmasters) that inevitably bleed together into what he calls the Complex Multiform Bullshit Job.

This is the job that looks as if it should be interesting because it is varied and yet stable, not routine or tenuous. But that is just bullshit about bullshit.

Not all bullshit jobs are boring jobs, but their capacity for inducing boredom is very high, simply because the meaninglessness of such work is so obvious. So while one can understand cheery business-magazine advice for the bored office worker – one such article advocates removing clocks, looking at animal pictures, using a sunlamp, and getting off envy-inducing social media – the smiley-face countermeasures are irrelevant to the gig-worker and bullshit job-holder alike.[61] Here the traditional political critique of boredom, with its roots in Marxist analysis, must be supplemented by the critical investigation of what I have been calling neoliberal boredom (section 5 below). Before that step, however, we must consider another form of boredom – or, more specifically, a form of boredom ideology – that seeks a positive spin on what is usually considered at best a painful affliction.

4 "Creative" Boredom

The emergent psychological literature is arguably a more scientific, but also more domesticated version of the sorts of claims made in section 1. That is, here boredom is understood as once more subjectively annoying but possibly productive. The natural adjunct to this literature is the rival psychological literature on the cognitive and even physical harms of boredom. Both of these rival, sometimes gridlocked, discourses tend to dominate in everyday discourse about boredom, especially with respect to technology, the built environment, and workplaces.

Consider, for example, one recent defence of boredom as ultimately enlivening, which argues that a little boredom goes a long way to making the world at large more interesting. "Boredom is understood as that frustrating experience of wanting but being unable to engage in satisfying activity," wrote Rosecrans Baldwin. "But it's an extremely short-lived emotion, and perfect for airports, sidewalks, afternoons in the woods. Maybe two minutes pass before I've found something worthy of note." Furthermore, "Something I've figured out in my boredom: To be at all smart, I need time to be stupid. Silent time – marked by barking dogs and traffic screeches and the murmurings of neighbors watching old movies. Time that's reserved to be listless and absent-minded not only reinvigorates my desire in being interested in things, it gives me the energy to be interesting, or at least try."[62]

Baldwin goes on to cite how his routine experiences of boredom – waiting in a line for bureaucratic service, for example – highlighted the pleasure he took in overhearing another person having a minor meltdown in the same setting. Most vividly, his everyday boredom leads him into an encounter with a crackhead screenwriter. Whether this counts as "creative" is of course open to debate.

The psychological literature has been more precise in its findings, but not much more illuminating about what counts as creative. Indeed, when we examine the psychological literature, we really see a therapeutic program to redeem boredom. By repositioning its presumptively negative features as opportunities for creative thought, boredom is effectively redefined (and defanged) as daydreaming, wool-gathering, brainstorming, and other "outside the box" or "lateral thinking" tactics. This tactical taming or domestication of boredom emerges as the opposite of philosophical boredom, which promises not future relief, but renewed anxiety. So-called creative boredom can take boredom only half-seriously.

5 Neoliberal Boredom

The pressing need for critical analysis of neoliberal boredom is rooted partly in perceived deficiencies of other literatures, but more seriously in the unremarked challenges to presumed-stable subjectivity that are alive in this evolving experience.

All of these accounts of boredom share this conviction: an ordinary, perhaps all too common human experience reveals some-thing larger. What the larger insight or insights might be is naturally a source of disagreement. My current argument engages that disagreement, but also suggests that, for too much of the literature, the focus of analysis is likely to be misplaced. The question is not so much, How is it that I come to be bored, and what does it mean that I am? The real question is, rather, Who is this "I" imagined to be the subject of boredom, and how did its existence come to be presumed in just this way?

Why "neoliberal"? Let us accept that neoliberalism is a valid term to describe a certain late-model version of capitalism. Liberalism *simpliciter* is the form of political organization that allows for differences in moral or religious belief to co-exist under shared minimal conditions. Above our many disagreements is an agreement, however tenuous, that we can tolerate differences in order to advance everyone's interests to the greatest possible degree. Neoliberalism emerges as a counter to, or third way between, these traditional liberal ideas of state organization and rival claims in favour of centralized, often socialist, government planning. In practice, neoliberalism as an ideology generates strong biases in favour of free markets, pooling of capital, and sector deregulation. The financial crisis of 2008 demonstrated for many the limits of this form of economic and political organization, but the general trend in favour of neoliberal ends has not significantly abated since then; indeed, depressingly, we have observed new and more creative forms of regulatory capture and, in the United States at least, a landmark Supreme Court decision that grants money free-speech protection, and hence political impact, under the Second Amendment to the Constitution.[63]

So what's boredom got to do with it? Well, my claim is that the peculiar form of boredom that now predominates in everyday cultural life, which is bound up with technological and economic realities, is in fact a political crisis of a new order. In addition, I claim that the crisis is intimately related to, and caused by, the background conditions of twentieth-century capitalism. Boredom is now a natural extension of the unease and restlessness generated in the economic sphere, everywhere exacerbated by upgrade imperatives, frenzied claims concerning speed and satisfaction, and perhaps worst, a constant generation of happiness-destroying envy for a form of existence that always seems to be elsewhere, enjoyed by someone else, or just past the horizon of the present in a future that never arrives.

This is consistent with a general sense of how capitalism has evolved during the past century and a half. Classical capitalism (1860–1930) is about the production of goods and services, the accumulation of wealth, and its expression in conspicuous consumption and demonstrations of waste in the form of privileged leisure. The cultivation of desire backed by such wealth provides an opportunity for integration of the self under the sign of taste. Veblen's dissection of the leisure class and the fiction of Edith Wharton are the keynotes here.[64] The central problem for this form of capitalism is that status goods such as the ones Veblen describes – fine wines, esoteric skills, art collections – are positional and so can't be equalized. Indeed, these are now often labelled Veblen goods, where their luxury status is denoted by a rising demand curve alongside a rising price curve, contrary to standard economic expectations. The situation of having highly desired but in-principle unequalizable goods is bound to create class tension and, eventually, social change in the form of graduated income taxes or widespread social reform such as the American New Deal (1933–36), which includes stiffer regulation and redistributive measures as well as national work projects.

The next discrete stage, late capitalism (1930–80), pivots on the production of consumption in the form of democratized "luxury" goods. Dissatisfaction and envy are countered by the spending and the shouldering of debt. Desire is manufactured by advertising efforts and popular culture, not simply cultivated as good taste for the few. Hence capital is reproduced rather than merely accumulated: the point of money is to spend it. The self here is fractured, but seeking a lost integration under the sign of happiness through such conspicuous spending. The textual-fictional compass points for this stage might be Adorno's and Horkheimer's analysis of "the culture industry," and the tragic-satirical fiction of F. Scott Fitzgerald.[65] The central problem is that the so-called democratic process, which reached a high point in social reform, gradually becomes indistinguishable from the culture industry itself. Politics is rendered into a form of entertainment, political battles into contests of war-chest capacity.

We are now, I suggest, enduring a third discrete stage that, for lack of a better adjective, we can call "postmodern" (1980–present). Here the cultivation of dissatisfaction is comprehensive, and desire proliferates in all directions. Capital is eroticized, a system of signifiers sustaining multifarious investments of desire without being itself real. Conspicuous leisure and conspicuous spending both give way to a pervasive drive towards conspicuous knowingness, early adoption, or hipness, especially if technological. The self is not merely fractured but, as we have seen, cannibalistic and spectral. Integration, which was still an assumed possibility under modern capitalist influence, is now impossible. Once more, textual reference is helpful: the cultural interventions of Žižek, perhaps, and the fiction of David Foster Wallace.[66] We no longer straightforwardly produce goods and services, or even produce consumption; instead, we produce and consume ourselves under the sign of our own status as consumers – or perhaps better "users," "followers," "friends," and so on. And yes, those scare quotes would seem to indicate the presence of word-casings in a particularly virulent form.

How depressing to realize that, so far from being exciting and fulfilling, the relentless spread of the desire-machinery has elicited boredom much more often. The reason is simple enough: the central features of this form of capitalism are (1) that it presents itself as inescapable and unique, unable to be replaced; but also (2), far worse, that it produces an endless series of zero-sum games involving our sense of entitlement to the wonders on offer. Sometimes, in a cruel irony, the opponent in such a zero-sum competition is my current self, facing off against an imagined future self.[67] The nascent sense that this is so, our own faint intimations of self-involved futility, lie at the root of neoliberal boredom. To see how and why this is so, I will now examine some examples of what I am calling the Interface, keeping in mind that these technological instances do not exhaust the range of Interface encounters or the extent of boredom that is possible under current conditions.

THE INTERFACE

Consider the following two parodies of a common activity in social media, particularly among young single people considering dates or relationships using apps such as Tinder, Match, or OkCupid. In an ad for the FX Network comedy *Man Seeking Woman*, the main character, played by Josh Greenberg, is seen in everyday situations: eating on his couch, sitting in his cubicle at work, using a urinal, waiting in line at a food truck. He suddenly senses something is wrong and then we see him hurtled bodily against the wall, through into the next apartment, or smashing into the truck. The scene then cuts away to a shot of two women, giggling over a smart phone as they somewhat gleefully flick his personal profile aside on the screen. We cut back to the scene at the food truck, where the hapless man's friend shakes his head sorrowfully and says, "Happens to the best of us."

The second example offers darker satire, as befits its source, the still occasionally wicked *Saturday Night Live*. In one of the show's pitch-perfect mock ads, a group of women are using a dating app called Settl. A roster of women discuss the "tons of OK dates" they've been on, realizing that "there's nothing wrong with the men on Settl. They're just normal guys with characteristics I am now willing to overlook." Photos of the men are restricted to passport shots or images of them standing next to the Tower of Pisa, because "that way, we can't focus on their looks." Maybe most tellingly, the spoof ends with a note that, unlike Tinder, Settl has no swipe-left function: "Because remember, it's not giving up. It's settling up."

The link between the spoofs is of course the very idea of the swipe rejection, something seen as all too easy in one instance – the feelings of usually unknown rejection being projected upon the fragile human individual – and as blocked in the other, because the illusion of choice suggested by swipe-left papers over a wealth of bad matches, handsome jerks, potential abuse, and all-too-common incivility and disappointment. As so often, the comedy here is a function of recognition: we all know, even if we are not seeking dates ourselves, the ruthless rules of the current mating rituals as mediated by omnipresent smartphones. Not to lean too hard on what is, after all, some rather ephemeral social commentary on a problem as old as humankind's sexual dimorphism, but it seems to me that the function and status of the swipe left is not sufficiently understood.

More recent coverage of dating patterns suggests that a reaction has already set in against online dating, especially app-based ones.[68] But the swipe remains, importantly, an example of how I understand the concept of *the Interface* in what follows. This is of course a term with various meanings, including ones that extend well beyond the graphic user interface (GUI) associated with contemporary computer and phone technology. I want to use it in a quite narrow and precise sense. The short version of my definition of the Interface is that it is fluid space that joins and allows interaction among platform, content, and user. Because it facilitates various kinds of threshold functions, the Interface is poorly understood just because, like physical thresholds, its importance is overlooked or taken for granted. What do I mean by that?

Recall the way Walter Benjamin, in beginning his well-known short essay on Kafka, uses the work of physicist Arthur Eddington to illustrate the feeling of Kafka's fictional world. "I am standing on the threshold about to enter a room," Eddington wrote in his best-selling 1935 book *The Nature of the Physical World*. "It is a complicated business."[69] Why? Well, for the attentive physicist the complications of this everyday act, blithely executed by ordinary humans a few dozen times in any given day, concern the implausible physical odds of such semi-conscious success. Much of the universe's entropic nature has to be organized precisely for one to pass without failure from one room to another. Molecules composed largely of empty space have to stay in good order for the affordances of stable floors and walls to admit of use. Our navigation of gravity and restricted space, performed from atop this peculiar upright two-footed stance, must be accurate.

Above all, we face the challenge of *mindedness* in our movements, the pursuit of goals and stimulus. (Eddington, a staunch believer in a pan-psychic universe, did not believe we moved around for no reason at all.) Indeed, this last achievement might be the most remarkable, since psychological studies reliably show that there is clear cognitive deficit experienced as one crosses thresholds. We forget what we were going to fetch, or lose track of the bright idea we came in here to note down.

Kafka's thresholds are, Benjamin suggests, the dark existential corollary to Eddington's physical mysteries. We are forever trying to open closed doors, climb a narrow staircase, or pass from one office to another. The mundane frustrations of physical life become, for Kafka, claustrophobic analogues of our social and mental anxieties, our inability to find peace and a sense of belonging in a world of doorways, offices, courts, and castles. The restlessness of Kafka's main characters, forever seeking an answer or a judgment beyond the next portal, or the next, is at once comical and fearsome, because those answers and judgments are never available; the doors that open do not lead us to where we wish to go, and the ones that remain closed are guarded by oddball gatekeepers and riddling tricksters. This is the human condition.

We may seem to have come a substantial distance from dating apps, but the darkness of the comic visions evident in the two spoofs indicates otherwise. Here we see the threshold function, which is typically experienced and deployed without conscious effort, revealed as violent or, perhaps worse, sending a message of acute despair when blocked. You can swipe, but you cannot hide – because it is you, and your desires, whom the swipe function at once serves and nullifies. Here, the user believes that he or she is engaging with the content (dating profiles) displayed on a platform (the site, with its ability to gather and display information). He or she also believes that the most important feature of this engagement is the exercise of judgment and choice, in rejecting or (sometimes) pursuing a possible dating contact. In fact, though, the most significant feature of the entire scene is not user, content, or platform, but instead the repeated finger-flicks of the swipe. The essence of the scene is the narrow way in which the user experiences himself or herself through the specific mechanism of this restless "choosing." That mechanism and a user's engagement with it is what I mean by the Interface.

Significantly this engagement can be at odds with the medium in which the user is immersed, and that helps us understand the distinction: the message of the medium is not identical with the message of the Interface. A recent example: in late 2017, a trend was identified of podcast listeners who, like quick-time scanners of magazine articles or blog posts, were playing the sound-based files or streams at 1.5, 2.0, or even 2.5 times the delivered speed. These people, labelled "podfasters," were responding to the large volume of things that they wanted to listen to by, in effect, accelerating the *rate of listening*.[70] The point was not to fast-forward through less-interesting sections of the piece in order to reach more interesting ones, the way one might use the relevant function to pass over commercials or dully rendered dialogue scenes in order to get to livelier material. It was, rather, to alter the experience of listening so that more could be heard in less time – often despite the wishes of the podcast creators, who might be employing music or deliberate pacing to create what they hoped were dramatic or intellectual effects. But alas for them, the user is in control of the Interface – or at least *imagines* that he or she is, given that the tools of the medium's end delivery are literally in their hands, on a phone screen or tablet. In fact, as we will see and probably suspect already, this feeling of controlling the experience is an illusion. And if neither the makers, the medium, nor the users are in control, then who or what is?

Let me posit a suggestion. Such *swipe-speed* mechanisms, as we might call them, take on a life of their own. Which is to say that, very soon, users begin to experience the scene not as one of judging and choosing profiles so much as one of engaging in the swipe or the hurry-up ingestion. That is why two (or more) people might enjoy the activity together, oblivious to the pain their happy-go-lucky game might cause to others. There is no actual pain, of course, because the profiles are not, in any real sense, actual people. The profiles exist, we might say, entirely to serve the interests of the mechanism of swiping. This is not the stated goal of such sites, to state the obvious, nor is it the reason most people enter into such engagements. My suggestion is that the Interface has an effect on presumed subjectivity – the supposed site of judging and choosing

– such that the subjectivity of the user is altered in ways that may not be evident to the user himself or herself, especially not immediately.

There is an analogue to addiction here, but it is only partial. An addict derives short-term pleasure from the satisfaction of his or her first-order desires. In many cases this first-order desire is at odds with a second-order desire not to fall prey, once again, to the allure of the drug or stimulus. But there are also cases of willing addiction and, more significantly, a strong element of temporality in the experience of addiction. This temporal dimension is far more complex than the usual short-term/long-term framework of crude addiction analysis. Desire for a given drug may wax and wane, may also be rationalized and resented in countless shades of nuance, before there is a definitive use of the drug or a confirmed judgment (whatever that might mean, exactly) that someone is an addict.

Neil Levy, for example, has argued persuasively that addiction is not incompatible with fairly robust conceptions of autonomy. "So why do addicts consume their drugs? The short and only somewhat misleading answer is that they take drugs because they want to," he writes. "The addict is not carried away by her desires in the way in which, in Aristotle's illustration of non-voluntariness, a man is carried across the road by the wind. The point is not that there is no such thing as compulsion by forces internal to the agent. The point is that, whether or not there are compulsive psychological forces, addictive desires are not among them."[71]

Levy does not deny that addiction is often unwanted, and harmful, or indeed that it is an impairment to full, flourishing autonomy. Rather, he argues that we should understand addiction as "characterized by an oscillation in the preferences of the addict. Most of the time, the addict sincerely disavows her addiction and wishes to be rid of it. But she regularly changes her mind; when she does, she genuinely prefers consumption to abstention."[72] This temporal aspect of addiction is too often neglected, as if the condition were a steady-state compromise of healthy desires by unhealthy ones. No, the addict is much more likely to experience deficits of healthy desire over time, impairing a global sense of self – what Levy calls "extended agency." This argument highlights less the failures of the addict to extend her will across time, though that is a valid description of addiction, and more the rarity of achieving globally healthy selfhood in the first place.

The Interface is not necessarily addictive, even in this autonomy-compatible sense, since it really functions as a deferral of desire-satisfaction *combined with* a substitution of its mechanism for the original desires that brought someone to the scene. This becomes evident when we compare other examples of the Interface, such as the search-library function available within music-storage sites or computer software. Here we can observe the very same restlessness and failure to choose associated with the dating apps. I scroll and scroll for something to listen to, but never settle on anything; soon the act of scrolling itself is the activity I am engaged in, which is offering me pleasure. A similar example is the constant scroll feature of online news sources, blogs, and (notoriously) Facebook, or the "next episode in *n* seconds" feature of Netflix. One can never come to the end of such experiences: there is always more being added to the feed – suggestive word! – and hence no opportunity for even the momentary sense of satisfaction experienced by the addict or, *a fortiori*, someone with a less troubled relation to his or her own desires.

The person caught up in the Interface is, in this sense, worse off even than the addict, at least those of the unwilling variant. The analogy to the willing addict is closest – though it is worth bearing in mind that the willing addict often looks a lot like a "healthy" person except for the adverse effects of the drug or stimulus. With many drugs, the maintenance of outward calm is part of the desired effect. But so, of course, is the pleasure of the drug itself. A character in Dan Kavanagh's 1987 novel *Going to the Dogs*, a former policeman, muses on the unsettling reality of addicts. "They do it because it's fun … It seems to you that the fun they get can't be worth it, you can see that it can't be worth it. To them it's worth it. You can call it addiction if you like, but you mustn't duck the other truth: they do it because it's fun."[73] Or, as the heroin-addicted narrator of Irvine Welsh's novel *Trainspotting* puts it: "People think it's all about misery and desperation and death and all that shite, which is not to be ignored, but what they forget is the pleasure of it. Otherwise we wouldn't do it. After all, we're not fucking stupid. At least, we're not that fucking stupid."[74]

What seems most prominent about the everyday experiences of the Interface is the fact that, despite the giggling over phones, they are not satisfying, even momentarily or at the expense of future well-being. The continuous nature of the scrolling or swiping seems to negate the very possibility of a satisfied desire. Instead, what we see here is desire out of gear – not in the sense of an impasse or stall, such as one might experience in procrastination, but rather in the way that an engine stuck in neutral can red-line its revolutions without producing any traction whatsoever. Eighteenth-century poet Edward Young called procrastination "the thief of time," an expression that has since become proverbial. When we put things off, we lose the apposite moment for productive action, even as we eat up the temporal fabric available in mortal existence. By contrast, in boredom time *hangs heavy on our hands*, as another saying has it. I watch the clock and wallow in uncertainty, waiting for something to happen. In such a state, to quote a more recent poet, Hal David, I just don't know what to do with myself. Time seems to flow too quickly in one condition, too slowly in the other. In fact, though, procrastination and boredom bear a structural affinity: in both cases desire cannot seem to fix itself on any given object or action. Both are forms of psychological conflict that influence our perception of the temporal. It is not without significance that Young's vivid expression comes in his mid-eighteenth-century poetry collection *Night-Thoughts*, a work known in its full title as *The Complaint: or, Night-Thoughts on Life, Death, & Immortality*. Elsewhere in the sequence, Young remarks that "wishing, of all employments, is the worst" – a grim assessment that is surely all the more true when what you wish for is a desire.

Once one is moved to evade the grip of boredom by further stimulus rather than reflection on the nature of the inner conflict, the swipe and scroll of Interface technologies offer repetitive actions that can have an almost mesmerizing effect on the user wrapped in the low-level rapture of desire-without-object. It is then no longer obvious just what harms this experience brings to the user, except perhaps in the obvious sense that she or he is devoting time to it that might be better deployed, even in her or his own terms, on something else. The relatively pleasant aspect of these engagements often masks a deeper issue, of course. I don't just mean the irony that the original desires – for a date, for some music to listen to, for an article or post to read online – are obliterated. It is also the case that the underlying restlessness of the Interface experience hides problems with world and meaning that are familiar to all students of boredom and its relation to happiness. Boredom is an emergent property of tangled desire. There is no more common, and no more distressing, condition known to humankind. Here, in our wishes and wants, our tortured souls erupt.

The structure of the Interface has now supplanted the role once played by content itself, such that our primary posture of consumption is no longer with the target material – whose delay or absence once promoted the experience of boredom – but with the mechanism of delivery. Boredom now consists not so much in "the paradoxical wish for a desire," as Phillips put it, but in the ever-renewable condition of no longer seeking a specific desire at all. The content has been superseded by the platform, and our immersion in the platform is, according to critic Nicholas Carr, a new form of consumption. "In a world dense with stuff," Carr writes, "a captivating Interface is the perfect consumer good. It packages the very act of consumption as a product. We consume our consuming." True enough; but so stated this claim does not go far enough. The perfect consumer good is not just the Interface, or even our consumption of consumption within it, but rather the self-devouring action of the immersion itself. This is the perfect consumption of *oneself* as perfect consumer.

The larger implications of this latter claim are just now beginning to reveal themselves, in particular those relating to selfhood and subjectivity. In our time, the fusion of technology, specifically media, with human subjects – more accurately, the subject positions of what Gilles Deleuze called *dividuals*, multiply divided selves – is a fact so central that, as in the parable of the fish who cannot know water, we are in danger of occluding the conditions of our being. Relations with the Interface, carried out on multiple platforms, become the sum total of the self's relation to its own conditions of possibility – but these conditions are thereby *rendered invisible*. Boredom is here best understood less as a disagreeable condition to be obliterated and more as a symptom whose mild discomfort signals a deeper malaise. We find we cannot easily live apart from the Interface, but also that the promises of the Interface – the content allegedly to be delivered by the platform – are a sly seduction. The Interface looms larger than content, but also larger than ourselves as we (so we believe) seek the content.

With a new sense of the stakes, revealed by analysis of the Interface-dominant features of neoliberal boredom, I propose that we may gain even greater insight about the various destabilized and spectral qualities of the "self" prone to prolonged sojourns with the Interface. Neoliberal boredom means not just the peculiar boredom of the Interface consumed in place of the content, but the distinct experience of *subjective emplacement* associated with that consumption – a species of imprisonment and lurking addiction in what turns out to be, indeed, rabid self-consumption.

Swiping will not solve the problem, for the problem is one that technology and the politics of consumption conspire to occlude. That occlusion, with its enabling political conditions, is the main subject of the present critical investigation. We turn next to the context that has made the condition of boredom so urgent for us now.

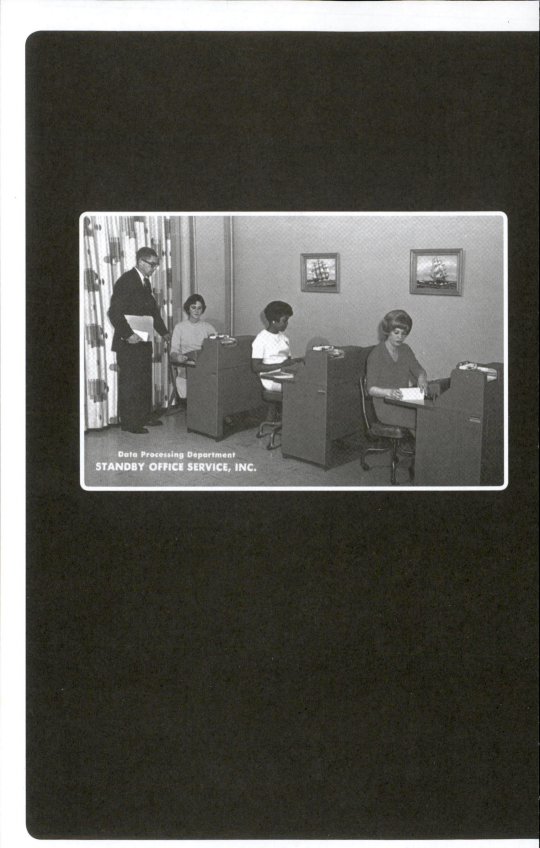

Data Processing Department
STANDBY OFFICE SERVICE, INC.

PART TWO

THE CONTEXT

MOOD REPORT

lonely,
frustrated,
full of ennui

Have you ever been so bored of yourself that you are
literally terrified? That is what it's like for me every day.
That is what it's like for me sitting here,
right now, right this second.

Jonathan Dee, *A Thousand Pardons* (2013)

LONELY

In order to understand the status of the Interface in our current predicament, we must isolate the effects of the "post-truth" condition, for these speak to both our sense of isolation *and* to the quiet desperation of wishing to overcome it through constant stimulation. It would be an error simply to identify post-truth failures with neoliberal economics, but there are suggestive linkages. In the neoliberal conception of value, all capital has the same status, covering over or cutting across any and all differences between people and even subordinating apparently robust political beliefs. A system that thrives on deregulation and competition, in allegedly "free" markets, generates in turn a cascading series of pathologies in public trust, public discourse, and public goods. It is not simply that we have, as the wry joke goes, the best government that money can buy; it is, further, that the usual justificatory mechanisms of liberal democracy are systematically hollowed out by monied interests, replaced by sham debate, accusations of "fake news," outright lies, and demented denials of the obvious. While the situation at the time of this writing offers an especially acute version, there is every reason to suppose that it is now endemic in political systems everywhere.

Samuel Johnson, writing in the *Idler* in 1758, noted, "Among the calamities of war may be jointly numbered the diminution of the love of truth, by the falsehoods which interest dictates and credulity encourages." The first part of Johnson's catalogue was shortened into US senator Hiram Johnson's more famous 1918 version: "Truth is the first casualty of war." The suggestion by both Johnsons is that wartime is an exceptional condition in which high stakes and high risk enable deterioration of otherwise healthy social and political norms. But what if the condition of war is ever-present, not merely in the factual sense that the United States, Britain, Canada, and other Western allies have been at war essentially since the first Gulf War began in 1990? It is also true that wartime measures, states of emergency and exception, and widespread surveillance have been normalized over the same period, and especially after the

New York and Washington terrorist attacks of 11 September 2001. And furthermore, during the same period we have witnessed a steep decline in standards of truthfulness among politicians, not least because the means and speed of fact-checking confident but false pronouncements are unsuited to the ceaseless news cycle and Twitter rants. The Interface is implicated in the breakdown of truth as a governing norm because it casts everything in a grey zone of zero accountability. By the time a falsehood has been noted, we are already three turns along in the cycle. And the cycle never stops.

How does this connect to the boredom I have associated with the Interface? Philosophers have typically believed that the truth can save us, even from the most severe depredations of our own faulty or perverted desires, and from the distorting influence of outside sources. That, indeed, has been the consistent promise of philosophical reflection, that it will *get things clear* in order that, should we be so minded, those things (false beliefs, muddy thinking, unjust systems, unethical practices) may be changed or discarded. But absent a norm of truth, can we even continue this illusion of therapeutic benefit from the philosophical analysis of boredom and its sources? There is no bright line between the erosion of truth as a public norm and the experience of neoliberal boredom, but the network connections between them can still be discerned. The ceaseless and depressing spectacle of political mendacity serves to isolate and immiserate citizens; as we have seen countless times, it even turns them against each other in violent ways. What counts as believable is governed by whether you watch Fox News, MSNBC, or CNN; by whose Twitter feeds you follow; by whom you choose to talk to on Facebook. There is tremendous loneliness and desolation in the political life of our time, and the lifebuoy of truth has disappeared beneath the waves. The boredom generated by such isolation is distinct from other modalities, as I have argued. It is restless, frustrated, sometimes angry; its sufferers are over-stimulated, not under-stimulated. They do not know what to do with their feelings, and, as so often, thwarted anger descends into depression. This is a problem that Heidegger and Schopenhauer apparently did not have to contend with!

Consider a tiny example. Everyone knows that campsite disputes can escalate, especially if brewed liquids are involved, but a 2016 dust-up near the small Canadian town of Brockville, Ontario, struck even seasoned campers as a little, uh, stupid. An argument over whether the Earth is round or flat prompted an angry man to toss a number of campsite items, including a propane tank, into a fire. He left the scene before firefighters arrived. It turned out the outdoorsy Flat-Earther is girlfriend to the tank-tosser's son – so, you know, family dynamics. Still, despite the existence of a whimsical society for people like her, we don't expect otherwise sane people to dispute centuries of scientific knowledge founded securely on the work of Pythagoras, Galileo, and Giordano Bruno. Or do we? Facts, truth, and evidence no longer exert the rational pull they once did. Our landscape of fake-news sites, junk science, politicians blithely dismissive of fact-checks, and Google searches that appear to make us dumber, render truth redundant. We are rudderless on a dark sea of confusion, disagreement, false flags, and memes.

We have been here before, of course, if not so comprehensively. Misinformation, rhetorical deceit, bogus belief systems, and plain ignorance are the norm, not the exception, in human affairs. But in most ages there has been a sense that this is a bad thing, something to be combatted actively. Plato acknowledged the sad dominance of *doxa*, or opinion, in everyday life. He countered with a stout defence of *episteme*, true knowledge, which philosophers alone could discern. Even philosophers no longer believe in that kind of philosopher, and the less modest notions of truth we have offered instead – pragmatic, empirical, falsifiable – can't halt cascades into skepticism and relativism. If it isn't divinely ordained or metaphysically copper-bottomed, truth looks like sick joke or power-grab, an epistemic cheque-kiting scam. Maybe Pontius Pilate was right to mock the idea rhetorically – "What is truth?" – and then not even tarry for an answer.

But the costs of giving up on truth are severe. In the perfervid summer of 2016, when this incident took place, it was hard to address any issue of public life without mentioning the presumptive Republican candidate for president of the United States, but President

Donald J. Trump really does represent a new stage of post-rational campaigning. The cynical, political-realist aides of George W. Bush argued that they created reality out of power. That position was doctoral-quality compared to the haphazard, say-anything approach of the new Republican regime. The shooter is an Afghan, even if born in New York! The president is a Manchurian-candidate ISIS mole! Muslims and Mexicans are – *you know!* What is significant is that rational push-back on this dangerous nonsense had so little traction during Trump's election campaign and now during his presidency. Correction used to cause shame and confusion; now it just prompts a rhetorical double-down. A lot of people are saying this! Actually important things – climate change, foreign policy – get dragged along for the moronic ride. For the record, yes, Hillary Clinton lied widely too in the election campaign, albeit with more consistency.

In the years following Trump's election in 2016, his random spew of half-truths and outright lies grew indiscriminately, like mushroom spoors in a cellar full of fertilizer. As David Remnick noted in the aftermath of the notorious July 2018 Helsinki "summit" with Russian president Vladimir Putin, where the crux of treason was apparently Trump's confusion over whether Russia "would be" or "wouldn't be" the obvious culprit in election meddling, the apparently endless spectacle of Trump getting away with his outrageous crookedness had become simply depressing. "Trump's penchant for bald deception and incoherence is not an aberration," Remnick wrote. "It is his daily practice. The vague sense of torpor and gloom that so many Americans have shouldered these past two years derives precisely from the constancy of Trump's galling statements and actions."[1] This, surely, is a new kind of boredom – the torpor of a depressed electorate that watches helplessly as its country is systematically undermined by a clear traitor who maintains a shadow-play of "putting America first" and "making America great again." Naturally the sham-show works beautifully at rabid rallies of the so-called Trump base and is unnaturally abetted by a spineless Republican Party that cannot dissociate itself from this obvious, indeed dementedly clownish whack-job for fear of surrendering its lucrative incumbencies.

A historical footnote worth mentioning: when Trump won the presidential election in 2016, a man named Erik Hagerman decided that he would go on a total media fast. No social media, no television, no radio, no internet. This action, undertaken on Mr Hagerman's pig farm in Ohio, was a conscious decision that is so unusual it elicited a long profile in the *New York Times*.[2] "It was draconian and complete," Hagerman said of his decision. "It's not like I wanted to just steer away from Trump or shift the conversation. It was like I was a vampire and any photon of Trump would turn me to dust." The semi-appalled *Times* reporter put it this way: "He has managed to become shockingly uninformed during one of the most eventful chapters in modern American history. He is as ignorant as a contemporary citizen could ever hope to be."

"I just look at the weather," said Hagerman, fifty-three, who lives alone. "But it's only so diverting." And then the key claims for our present purposes: "I am bored," he said. "But it's not bugging me." The *Times* writer Sam Dolnick spotted the true stakes: "It takes meticulous planning to find boredom," he wrote. "Mr Hagerman commits as hard as a method actor, and his self-imposed regimen – white-noise tapes at the coffee shop, awkward scolding of friends, a ban on social media – has reshaped much of his life." Of course it has. But is this a luxury lifestyle for the financially blessed? Hagerman is a former executive for Nike, who can afford a media blackout just when others might find it impossible. His boredom is a Veblen good, priced out at a point where most consumers cannot go. It bears some relation to creative boredom as set out earlier, but also has elements of the specifically neoliberal condition now rendered from burden to pleasure. This is very advanced boredom thinking – in short, a form of self-conscious turtling that renders the outside world null. Truth no longer matters to the person who has retreated inside his shell; neither, by the same token, do the lies and bullshit whose cumulative effect is the erosion of rationality itself.

Alas, philosophical claims for the authority of reason have always been more hopeful than stable. There is, we want to say, a basic regard for truth in making any claim, however bizarre or unproven. Watching the nightly pundit-parade or the scroll of toxic opinionating, we have cause to doubt it. This is the carapace of reason, a shell of discourse preserved in debate-club tactics and the collective delusion that this constitutes discourse. We must distinguish, as Martin Luther did, two kinds of reason (though he got the priority wrong). Ministerial reason deploys argument-forms in the service of existing belief, convincing someone else that I will not be convinced otherwise. Magisterial reason, by contrast, is autonomous: it engages in dispute openly to pursue – if not always find – the truth. If evidence and argument are contrary to my pre-existing beliefs, reason demands that I change them.

Meanwhile, for those tracking these things, Google, Facebook, and Amazon are getting smarter by the day. Their advanced algorithms, which track and gather data in the form of your search queries, friend requests, or shopping preferences, can generate new results that characterize you with astonishing, or perhaps frightening, accuracy. At a certain point the algorithm knows me better than I know myself – not least because, per Deleuze's insight about *dividuals*, it is less and less clear that our cherished unique and inward selves are anything more than these queries, requests, and preferences. Algorithms this advanced constitute a new form of artificial intelligence, using our own immersion in technology against us. The only choice when it comes to corporate entities like these – so apparently inextricable from everyday life as privileged people now live it – is blanket refusal. You can't selectively offer your data to Amazon: every item you purchase is a data point for further analysis against your previous and future ones, and all of everyone else's previous and future ones.

One might follow the path of such refusal, but Amazon is dedicated to making itself indispensable to your life, offering more and more items for sale, delivering them in some cases within hours, even (with your permission) opening the door to your house to leave them safe in your absence. Refusal begins to look a lot like deprivation when one has become accustomed to the swooping A to Z arrow of the company's logo, which looks suggestively like a puckish smile. These various services have provided Amazon founder Jeff Bezos a personal net worth, as of 2018, of US$143.1 billion. I found that figure by doing a Google search, of course. Research without Google is now almost inconceivable, even for traditionalists like me. It is just too easy to use the very same screen on which I am writing this to call up a browser window and check on spelling, a fact, or a reference I cannot clearly recall. Once more, there is no option to limit or filter my data. (I can clear my browser history but the searches are already logged elsewhere.)

Even as outward searches and requests are being monitored and pumped into choice-determining programs, technology from the same companies is being brought into our homes. What started with clunky smart TVs and refrigerators with internal monitors to check on food freshness has been transformed into the ubiquitous voice-activated personal assistant who will provide whatever you wish for – at the cost of recording what you say. Amazon's Echo technology, otherwise known as Alexa, as well as Google Assistant and the semi-successful Apple Siri have taken hold of the imagination of consumers everywhere, answering verbal requests for music, phone calls, channel changes, movie tickets, weather reports, dinner reservations, and more. At the time of writing this remains a relatively scarce luxury good, and one whose marginal costs of lost privacy and vertical integration seem inconsiderable to happy users. One recent ad touting the system shows an extremely well-off family, ensconced in a warmly lit mountainside Modernist house straight out of the pages of *Architectural Digest*, reacting with glee as the invisible servant-surveillance-agent responds to their every whim. The father, salt-and-pepper handsome in his fifties, chuckles with delight. As a vision of happiness its message could not be clearer: the seamless integration of close family, material comfort, desire fulfillment, and good cheer, all enabled by the system recording your conversations and tracking your choices. Clearly anyone who lacks this household miracle must be a loser.

Of course, as we know, technology becomes rapidly less marvellous through use, and the wonder of today is the forgotten furniture of tomorrow. We all know that our screens are everywhere dominant: they (pick your macabre metaphor) are vampires, or drug pushers, or zombification viruses. Americans spend on average three to four hours a day looking at their phones, and as much as eleven hours a day in front of screens of all kinds. The next revolution, therefore, must involve a move away from screens and into total immersion. And so, as we arguably reach a "peak-screen" moment in 2018 we enter a near-future in which internet technology blankets the home, street, and office. The Interface is now *our entire environment*. It is literally in the air. No, better: it *is* the air, the air of instant gratification that we breathe every day. One booster for the coming shift, Farhad Manjoo, notes that screenless personal assistants offer "something new: a mobile computer that is not tied to a huge screen, that lets you get stuff done on the go without the danger of being sucked in. Imagine if, instead of tapping endlessly on apps, you could just tell your AirPods, 'Make me dinner reservations at 7' or 'Check with my wife's calendar to see when we can have a date night this week.'"[3] Yes, just imagine that!

The striking thing about the rhetoric in favour of the totally immersive tech-vironment is how it combines a sage warning with deceptively innocuous new moves in Interface dominance. "Screens are insatiable," Manjoo argues. "At a cognitive level, they are voracious vampires for your attention, and as soon as you look at one, you are basically toast." And indeed, studies show that cognitive capacity is reduced by the mere presence of a smartphone in the vicinity of a habitual user. Many tech critics have begun to speak seriously of the addictive features embedded in screen time, as well as the economic and personal costs of allowing yourself to be held hostage to some of the richest companies in history. "Your phone is so irresistible that when you can see it, you cannot help but spend a lot of otherwise valuable mental energy trying to not look at it," Manjoo warns in the now-familiar fashion. He suggests that the possible solutions are two-fold. First option: exercise willpower in resisting the phone, possibly with the help of meta-technology designed to limit your access. Screen Time, for example, is a feature that shows you just how much time you are spending on the phone and can even block your access to certain apps. Other site-blocking apps include Freedom, Self-control, AppDetox, cold turkey, Block Site, and StayFocusd. More recent self-control apps include Moment, which also measures screen time, and Forest, a graphic app that grows a healthy tree on your screen when you are not using it – which then withers to dust the instant you pick up the device again.

Of course we know that the mind is weak, so willpower alone probably won't break your addictive cycles. An anonymous psychology professor, quoted in a 2018 newspaper article, noted that the struggle here is essentially one of virtue against vice: we want to create long-term goods by curbing short-term pleasures. Before phone apps there were (and are) self-control mechanisms such as buying one cigarette at a time to cut back on chain-smoking or putting your alarm clock in the room next to the bedroom, forcing a waking walk. We might go further and lock away temptations or perform acts of violence such as self-flagellation. The problem with all these mechanisms is that, like the addiction itself, they generate tolerances over time: the self-control mechanism becomes so comfortable it is no longer effective. Asked by the reporter what she does herself to combat her own phone addiction, the professor confessed. "I might not be a good example," she said. "When I have a really big paper to write, I change all my passwords to random digits I won't remember." She paused. "Then I hide it in a drawer." Another, longer pause. "I hide it in a drawer at home so that even if I want to check at work, I won't be able to. I just don't trust myself or my self-control. So I've decided to just be realistic about it."[4]

This lack of self-trust, so common with addictions both mild and severe, eats away at the advice of tech-savvy skeptics like Jaron Lanier, the digital pioneer who has lately become a fervent critic of social media. His 2018 book *Ten Arguments for Deleting Your Social Media Accounts Now* is just that – a series of arguments.[5] That is to say, they are rational claims aimed at rational actors, who might be motivated by self-interest rather than sweet reason itself, but who are nevertheless open to persuasion. Any injunction to self-control based on argument depends for its force on the agent being already receptive to the idea of media avoidance, and having sufficient self-control to execute the strategy. Meanwhile, the craving for online "connection" continues to breed alienation and polarization, false notions of popularity, and massive data scoops for the private interests that actually control apparently public forms of communication. As Lanier says, all social-media use, even when apparently benign, generates net losses in human "dignity, happiness, and freedom." If only realizing that were enough (spoiler alert: it's not). Something Lanier does not mention is that social-media harms are not consistent across populations, with some aspects – relentless anxiety about social status, for example – disproportionately affecting young women over young men.[6]

So second option, then, at least for some: change the drug. "[A] digital ecosystem that demands less of our eyes could be better for everyone – less immersive, less addictive, more conducive to multitasking, less socially awkward, and perhaps even a salve for our politics and social relations," Manjoo enthuses. But these far-flung claims are hard to credit: why should we imagine that the solution to too much tech is more tech? How, exactly, is a voice-activated personal-assistant technology with its "quick hits" of search and plan "less immersive" and "less addictive" than the soul-sucking screen? True, visual stimulus is probably the strongest kind we experience; but at least with a screen you know you're a slave to your addiction and the attention-economy corporate interests who enable it. When the corporation's agent is welcomed inside the home as a sort of benign and ever-present digital butler, the smooth integration of soul and software seems complete. Despite the tone of revolutionary fervour in this analysis – the word *revolution* is mentioned in the headline – there is little concrete sense of how new levels of ubiquitous connection would provide a "salve" for politics and social relations, which are indisputably tainted by technology now in the form of social media. How, precisely, would non-screen networking help? Would Alexa vote for us, or lobby on our behalf? One can be forgiven for concluding cynically that the only revolution in play here is the usual one of the already-dominant tech giants offering us just one more new toy to play with.

And finally, let's be honest: even if I were to offload all mundane tasks to Alexa or Siri, I would still have lots of vulnerable cognitive capacity left over to be obliterated by games and pointless but compelling apps. The screen has not peaked. Addiction still stalks the tasty meat of our brains by way of our eyes. (I will have more to say about addiction in part 3.)

Not every user of these tools is bored and lonely, of course, any more than every participant on social media is a troll. But technology is never neutral. Its tendencies and biases, often erased through ease of use and growing familiarity, in fact condition our responses and reactions, even shape elements of our unsettled subjectivity. There is a promise of meaning and connection in the time and typing we offer to the websites of our everyday lives. We are, in the verbed form of the Interface's favourite noun, *friending*. But the keyboard's promise of meaning, like art's promise of happiness, seems forever deferred in its fulfillment.[7] Sometimes we turn to the screen out of boredom; but just as often, if not more so, we find there only the grinding boredom of the scroll itself – distraction once more flees itself into distraction. This will not change even if we move from screens and keys to voice commands. The ever-stronger artificial intelligences enabled by our own bestowals of attention, our sad need to connect to something, even if it's just an Amazon purchase or random tweet, will encounter little resistance from such half-persons. Suffused with an ennui we cannot alleviate through more stimulation – our mental fluids being already supersaturated – we will offer easy pickings to entities with more purpose and coherence. We have, after all, accepted this imprisonment willingly already. Loneliness begets loneliness in a shadow-play of promised connection.

People always say, at this point, that such concerns are paranoid, even a form of fear-mongering. If you don't have anything to hide, why fuss about surveillance? If you like to have shopping suggestions made for you by an algorithm that tracks your every move, what's the problem? Maybe we should stop worrying and welcome our new shopping-site and search-engine overlords! Or maybe, instead, we should recall that rational thought really just means this: an ongoing agreement to try to take each other seriously, especially when the condition of the self can seem so wispy and ephemeral, reduced to apps, hits, DMs, and search terms. The self reduced to a series of heedless rises to click-bait needs more truth, not less.

In the age of "alternative facts" and post-truth conviction – which is to say, conviction without foundation – we must counter the pervasive influence of the Interface in all its forms with a renewed dedication to the normativity of truth. But the standard view of philosophical criticism as ultimately revelatory will also have to be modified to cope with the current socio-political context and our consumer-citizen status within it. This may prove difficult, but I promise it won't be boring.

It is not precisely that people are so bored by the enervating spectacles of the twenty-four-hour news cycle that they ratchet up their own convictions to make politics more to their liking – though there is some truth to this account. It is more the case, I think, that the shared civic seems more and more drained of sustainable meaning, and hence pitches us back with force on our own, often meagre, inner resources. The relationship to boredom should become obvious. When words and statements no longer mean what they used to or have only free-floating "alternative" meanings depending on the moment, we are in a crisis of meaning – what political theorist Michael E. Gardiner calls *semiocapitalism*. Although traditional critics of late-modern capitalism "talk about such affective states as anxiety, depression, indifference or panic in relation to" the halting formation of subjectivity under capitalist conditions, "they do not address in any sustained fashion what many regard as the most common mood or affect of our times – namely, that of boredom."[8] Boredom, "understood as a tangible if characteristically ambivalent (and ambient) mood or affective condition that relates to modes of capitalist production in specific ways," must be addressed in new ways. Specifically, Gardiner's argument aligns with my own that there is a form of twenty-first-century boredom that is new and deeply entwined with those "modes of capitalist production," including the endless feed of the media cycle, where not only is debate absurdly bifurcated into squabbling us-versus-them panels, but where the chief executive of an otherwise serious nation can engage in systematic gaslighting of the entire population. "Just stick with us," President Trump enjoined supporters in a July veterans' rally during the 2018 trade war. "Don't believe the crap you see from these people, the fake news. Just remember: what you're seeing and what you're reading is not what's happening."

In what way, then, can we say that truth is dependent upon interpretation without descending into semiocaptialist chaos? An orthodoxy of a certain brand of hermeneutics and critical theory would argue that truth always depends upon context. The validity of claims is determined by the contours of a given interpretive frame or method, which generate the sorts of truth-claims that will count as valid within a given discourse. This view, not in fact postmodern as sometimes charged but rather high modern, is what people often attack as "relativism" or "subjectivism" concerning truth. It is of course no such thing, since context-dependence forbids the comparison of truths from different contexts that would make them equally and compatibly true (what most people mean by relativism), while also ruling out accounts of the world based entirely on a single point of view (what most people mean by subjectivism). Meanwhile, cynical appropriations of allegedly postmodern notions by right-wing political apparatchiks are consistently revealed as cynical and self-serving, not honest or liberatory. And they are certainly not the responsibility of left-wing critics who brought the ideas to bear on reified structures of power and belief in the first place.[9]

The ethical and political implications of this epistemological dispute have long been noted. Are there standards of action and judgment that are true, or are there just conventions that vary between cultures? Can we decide matters of behaviour and evaluation according to a reliable objective standard, or will we always find ourselves mired in endless irresolvable disputes? So stated, this is a false dichotomy concerning the issue of normative evaluation. There can be standards of judgment that are action-guiding and reliable, even as they forbear from pretending to universal or extra-human status. We need not purchase ethical life at the cost of committing to an objectivist position. Contextualism offers one promising route away from this otherwise crippling dichotomy, and I will explore and defend a version of it in what follows. The subjective-objective bind proves to be a self-imposed imprisonment, one from which we can free ourselves without courting incoherence or anarchy.

Even more interesting in the present moment, however, are the political implications of context-dependence. If the "postmodern" left was accused of making truth subservient to political ends in an overt ideological fashion, it has been in fact the political right that has achieved this spectral triumph. The obvious focal point of this appropriation is the once-anonymous quotation, now reliably attributed to George W. Bush strategist and chief of staff Karl Rove, that most people reside "in what we call the reality-based community," which Rove defined as people who "believe that solutions emerge from your judicious study of discernible reality ... That's not the way the world really works anymore. We're an empire now, and when we act, we create our own reality. And while you're studying that reality – judiciously, as you will – we'll act again, creating other new realities, which you can study too, and that's how things will sort out. We're history's actors ... and you, all of you, will be left to just study what we do."[10] Postmodern right-wing *realpolitik* thus creates "realities," "facts," and (crucially) perverse accusations of "fakeness" in pursuit of a specific political agenda. Perhaps the most surprising thing about this for many people today is that it by no means began with Trump, unlikely forty-fifth president of the United States.

DOOMED WISH

The most basic and most erroneous assumption of untutored discourse about discourse, especially of the political kind, is that there is a firm distinction between "the facts" or "the fact of the matter," on the one hand, and the various, perhaps competing interpretations of those facts on the other. The assumption represents a mistake of presumption, namely that interpretations supervene on a baseline reality that, at best, can be discerned through effort and methodology, perhaps via triangulation among competing interpretations; and further that the baseline reality, once so discerned, will prove decisive in whatever matter is at hand. Consider, for example, the experience of watching Akira Kurosawa's classic 1950 film *Rashomon*. Here, in chilling near-repetition, we are exposed to rival and contradictory versions of the "same" series of events, involving a rape and murder in the Japanese countryside. But the four accounts, given in turn, prove self-serving, strange, and inconclusive.

What are we to make of this? Is the truth of what happened something that matches none of the narratives perfectly, but has elements of truth from each? Or is there a further ur-narrative that none of the individuals can recount but that, from a god's-eye (or viewer's, or director's) perspective, can be made out? Maybe, most disturbingly, there is no truth here at all, in the sense of a stable array of actions and reactions, motives and consequences. Naturally the last possibility is both the most probable and the most important: human affairs, especially extreme ones, do not surrender to our assumptions about "making sense" of "what happened." The film works to both highlight and undermine the assumption, and its critical logic is of a piece with what we might call the *unveiling* function of modern critical theory. What is unveiled is not the truth, but instead our fervent but doomed wish for there to be such a thing as the objective truth that chases all rival accounts from the field. Such a wish is, we might say, a form of Platonic-Cartesian hangover, an understandable but unrealizable desire to off-load responsibility for our own beliefs and actions to a higher power. In its own way, the enduring longing for capital-*T* Truth is not unlike the unwilling addict's fervent desire to be delivered from his own responsibility. Alas it is not that simple. Epistemological deliverance is not on the cards.

And so I align this aesthetic intervention of a film with contemporaneous critical theory for several reasons. First, we can see here how in the mid-twentieth century there operated an intellectual consensus about what we might call the duty of exposure. By this I mean the impulse shared by Nietzschean-Marxist-Freudian hermeneutics of suspicion: in very broad terms, thoughts are never innocent, ideology functions everywhere, and we suppress awareness of our own suppressions. The critical intervention then takes the form of showing what has been hidden, exposing comforting social conventions, political self-deception, and psychological repression, respectively. Everyday society and psychology alike work to maintain illusions that are conciliatory and serving the interests of the current arrangement. The duty of exposure meets this shell game of falsity by leveraging penetrating insight and an unwillingness to take the taken-for-granted for granted.

I label this impulse high modern because it is fundamentally implicated in a larger project of Late Enlightenment. In fact, though, this implication has a long and complicated pedigree, especially in politics and philosophy. We can certainly trace it back to Kant's well-known injunction in "What Is Enlightenment?" – *sapere aude* (have the courage to think for yourself) – but we could equally follow a longer and somewhat crooked line that would trace its way to Socratic *elenchus* and the exposure of false consciousness in the words and concepts of everyday life. Philosophy in its basic critical mode, in short.

But the ground here is, not surprisingly, unstable, and that generates a second reason to implicate the "Rashomon effect" in our account of post-truth. According to communications theorist Robert Anderson, whose work has popularized the term, "the Rashomon effect is not only about differences in perspective. It occurs particularly where such differences arise in combination with the absence of evidence to elevate or disqualify any version of the truth, plus the social pressure for closure on the question."[11] The last qualification is essential, since it illustrates how the multiple-interpretation experience is *both* destabilizing *and* driven towards a new moment of new stability. This "closure" can no longer claim the mantle of baseline reality associated with the untutored or naive view of "what happened," but it nevertheless exerts a normative force of consensual order.

Thus the very same impulse that forces us to confront our hidden assumptions and ideological pre-commitments must recognize, sooner or later, the second-order problem of its own assumptions and pre-commitments. At its most obvious, insufficiently self-reflexive critical theory generates a performative contradiction, whereby the exposure of what lies hidden results in a reification of the exposure. In crude terms, the work of showing "what is really going on" simply falls into a trap of reactionary ontological conviction. Instead of the naive realist view of the world as we find it, we adopt an "enlightened" view of the world as self-deceived. But that latter is as much committed to the notion of baseline reality as the former.

Less obviously, the status of the exposure efforts may prove itself uncertain: what is gained, after all, by bringing to the surface ideas and commitments that were hitherto buried? (The images of surface and depth are rife in the literature, of course; Freud's famous image of the iceberg, with some 85 per cent of the psyche "under water," is memorable here.)

Hence, as awareness of these tangles becomes more inescapable, theorists begin to make a genuine postmodern turn. By this I mean the traditional "incredulity towards metanarratives" that Lyotard identifies in his work, but also those reversions to simulacral logic that are prompted by a crisis of faith in the standard critical-theoretic project. One can observe the problem already in the late work of Adorno and even (though less vividly) in Barthes: if the work of theory is to reveal by de-naturalizing assumptions and power relations, how do we avoid simply valorizing the revealed condition as *more true*?[12] Adorno labelled the basic project one of "seeing-through," and he was rightly troubled by its potential tangles and endgames. That is, the logic of revelation seems to carry with it an *implicit reification of the (now) seen* that is impossible to evade. Only a principled refusal of this logic can suffice in maintaining a critical attitude. And, notably, the function of criticism must now shift, because there is no longer any possible claim to authoritative interpretation, nor indeed a claim to the assumed hierarchical relation of interpretation to thing interpreted. It is, we might say, interpretation all the way down. This does not surrender the idea of normativity in knowledge and belief; in anything, it sharpens the point of criticism. As I will conclude in part 4, the constant stimulation of the Interface can be countered only by a project of constant philosophical criticism: this is one key insight illuminated when neoliberal boredom is transformed into philosophical boredom.

Of course, Nietzsche himself had glimpsed this insight about the limits of epistemology in the much-quoted passage concerning facts and interpretations ("There are no facts, only interpretations"). But in a crucial sense Nietzsche did not take his own insight seriously enough, or perhaps he was too addicted to the pleasure of the intellectual reveal to commit to it completely. By the middle of the following century, Barthes and others had added the structuralist apparatus of linguistics to their cultural-critical toolkit, but still without abandoning a project of penetrative insight. Of his ground-breaking 1957 work in the study of popular culture, *Mythologies*, Barthes wrote, "This book has two determinants: on the one hand, an ideological critique of the language of so-called mass culture; on the other, an initial semiological dismantling of that language: I had just read Saussure and emerged with the conviction that by treating 'collective representations' as sign systems one might hope to transcend pious denunciation and instead account in detail for the mystification which transforms petit bourgeois culture into a universal nature."[13] We see here a standard (and persuasive) account of the reveal project. Barthes always wishes us to see what has been encached in the "mystifications" of cultural production and consumption. Thus the de-mystification project, which will presumptively reverse the transformation of particular (petit bourgeois) interests into universal (natural) norms by showing precisely their origins, limits, and political tendencies. We are still in the realm of Socrates.

Adorno had of course struggled with the same commitments, though he is considerably less consistent in avoiding the "pious denunciation" that Barthes sees as unhelpful in this quarter. Adorno knew that his dyspeptic critiques of camping, sunbathing, television, radio, jazz, and movies (among other things) were reactionary. He also came to know, rather more reluctantly, that these critiques were pointless. If Barthes senses that denunciation is not the point, understanding is, Adorno simply abandons any stance other than the "get off my lawn" crankiness of a man out of joint with his time and place.

Only Debord and Baudrillard, it seems to me, really perceive the extent of the difficulty here.[14] We must take seriously the idea that there are no facts of the matter, that culture is not a shell game working to prop up articulable bourgeois interests, but instead a free play of empty signifiers and random spectacles that – yes – tend to reinforce current interests, but not by hiding a discoverable truth.

Indeed, the basic truth is there for all to see: *there is no definitive truth in play!* There really are only interpretations, and semi-random arrangements of cultural properties that suggest or provoke but never – can never – speak plainly. The people who understand this are the true postmodernists, those who do not subconsciously revert to a truth-revealing logic of emancipation, but instead accept that the distinction between reality and fantasy is not stable, perhaps does not exist at all.

What this means politically, of course, is that the comprehensive triumph of spectacle renders moot all other scales of evaluation, even as it promises to banish all boredom in a play of constant media stimulation. The advent of the "reality television" chief executive is a predictable symptom of an epistemological system in which truth and falsity are indistinguishable. One may tarry on the structural conditions that make these erasures possible – erosion of traditional authority, wide dissemination of social media, encroachments on the phenomenology of "real life" – but they all point to the same conclusion. We can no longer reliably separate truth from falsity, reality from appearance. The longstanding Western philosophical project has reached its endgame, and its results are in: not only can anyone say anything, but the anyone saying anything can be the highest elected official in the most powerful nation on Earth. Welcome to the postmodern condition!

GETTING REAL

Of course nothing is quite that simple in the realm of human affairs – or, indeed, in the realm of epistemology. Many people see in President Trump a primitive mendacity that is more primordial, appealing to the reptile brain of those who find pleasure in the basic logic of us versus them. (This can be, to be sure, a more sophisticated political force too: compare Carl Schmitt's nuanced realist political philosophy of friend and enemy.[15])

"Where do Donald Trump and other world authoritarians fit into the history of facts?" critic Ian Brown asked. "It's fashionable these days to claim that Mr Trump and his ilk are super-sophisticated 'post-truth' types, that they have expropriated the terrain of postmodernism and seized the handy high ground where everything is relative, where the truth is simply what you can convince people of." Brown begged to differ: "Within the history of facts, the 45th president is actually a throwback, an atavist of a more primitive consciousness. And it is digital-information technology that has allowed him to be that way."[16] Brown even feels the need to repeat the claim, saying that "it's important to understand Donald Trump within the context of the history of facts. He's not a sophisticated post-factual postmodernist. He's a throwback, not just beyond the rationality of Voltaire to the emotionalism of Rousseau, but way, way, waaaaaay back, to pre-Enlightenment mystical shamanism, to the credulous world of shadows inside Plato's cave, to abracadabra and the wowza flash of fire."

The *apparent* pre-modernism of Trump is in fact a property emerging from right-wing postmodern conditions. Granted, Trump is more the unwitting beneficiary of these conditions than the conscious creator thereof. But his abilities *not to regard facts*, or to rely on *alternative* ones, are essential to his success. Perhaps the pre-modern media-age avatar is just the logical extension of the new postmodern condition? This is especially evident in his preferred medium of communication, Twitter, which relies on reaction and brevity, even in the revised 280-character version. Twitter is a force amplifier, but one with special features that make for political separation and epistemological confusion. People choose whom they will follow, and competitive economies of followers immediately ensue: a potentially toxic popularity contest, which the president wins before even playing his next move. There is no possibility of linear thinking or sustained argument. And, as with all phone- or screen-based media, the interaction is isolated even as it feels connected. Piling on is common, in part because it is not centrally directed: many people issue the same denunciation (or, more rarely, praise) without consulting anyone else. Each Twitter user speaks with the voice of authority born of that same isolation. Fortunately most users don't have access to deployable nuclear weapons; unfortunately, one of them, and indeed one of most unhinged and petulant, does.

Because postmodernism has traditionally been associated with the left, we must be ever-mindful of the radical co-optations of the ideas by the imperial right or, more lately, the populist-isolationist right. One might be tempted to dismiss the talk, quoted earlier, of empire-created realities as typical Karl-Rovean bluster; and indeed the defeat of the Republicans in the 2008 presidential election gave many people hope that the imperial "Mission Accomplished" posturing of the Bush administration was a thing of the past, an aberration. But I tend to credit Rove with a deeper insight here, namely that his diagnosis is correct, even in the absence of an American imperial mission. Rove understood, in other words, that the new millennium had generated new norms of political discourse and behaviour. The old pieties of Enlightenment thought, including the essential premises that there is such a thing as "reality" penetrable by reason, and that such penetration has the power to alter behaviour, were in the dustbin of history. In their place was the *postmodern right-wing realpolitik we have come to know all too well*, the conviction that power ("action" in Rove's formulation) creates its own rules and (temporary) realities. Morphed into the circus populism and complete shamelessness of the next Republican administration, these factors cook up a potent stew of fear, mistrust, and confusion – not to mention boredom at the relentlessness of the string of new outrages. Those of us still trapped in the norms and methods of the "reality-based community" can now only stand by and watch, no doubt wringing our hands all the while. Our sharp tools of the mind, the honed chisels of evidence and logic, are just so many parlour tricks – and worse, ones whose unexamined exercise results only in pulling the wool over our own eyes.

The 2010 *Citizens United* decision has had equally dire consequences, though they tend to arrange themselves outside the evening news shows and Twitter rants of current political reality. In the view of the Court, based on an interpretation of the US Constitution's Second Amendment, restrictions on independent corporate expenditures in political campaigns, as opposed to direct political contributions, are unconstitutional restrictions on the freedom of speech. This decision at once inhibits democracy by quantifying (and then hiking) the opportunity costs of participation, even as it reduces the idea of such participation to money itself. To be sure, corporations have been granted some of the rights of citizens in American law for some decades. But *Citizens United* does more than extend such rights. By means of a spectral metaphysics of plutocracy, it effectively delivers the electoral process over to the moneyed interests whose pools of capital are now instantly transformed into pools of influence.

These artifacts of recent political history might seem unrelated, and yet, in the context of standard liberal views on pluralism, civility, and integrity, they are not only related but matters of the utmost urgency. Alasdair MacIntyre, in his 1981 book *After Virtue*, argued that a viable virtue ethic required not just an enumeration of desirable character traits, or dispositions to act, but also, crucially, two other features.[17] First, there must be a sense of a *role* that one could legitimately play, a virtuous identity, such as the Aristotelian *phronimos*, the Augustan gentleman, or the thrifty New Englander; and second, there must be a suitable background *context* for the exercise of the enumerated virtues, a set of shared assumptions that would assure the reinforcement cycle between action and character.

The presumption of virtually all philosophical argument concerning civility and pluralism, whether one takes an explicitly virtue-style account or not, is precisely that there is such a context: public reason, courts of reasonable appeal, individuals with preferences to articulate, and so on. But what if the context is in fact one where these presumptions are maintained only as fictions, where the real influence and even the notion of speech has been stealthily – and not so stealthily! – removed from the hands of individual citizens and placed, instead, in spectral agencies or pools of power in the form of money?

We cannot go on, it seems to me, without addressing these practical realities of civic life, and the way they are replicated over and over by our immersion in the boredom-banishing devices of everyday existence. Social media have proven worse than inadequate as a substitute for robust public discourse, instead inviting tirades, rant, and storms of violent reaction to the events of the day. The very tools we come to depend on as amplifiers of our individual insignificance or respite from our torpor have had, in the event, the countervailing effect of hollowing out community and increasing disconnection. Defenders of civility may therefore need to abandon the optative, restraint-based accounts that have hitherto dominated and instead seek routes of argument that include analysis of systematic discursive distortions, once thought – by Habermas, for example – to be the exclusive preserves of ideology or madness. Meanwhile, as we know only too well, the very idea of "civility" is a rant-worthy hot-button concept. In the summer of 2018, for example, when White House press secretary Sarah Huckabee Sanders, a notoriously evasive and hostile shill for the Trump administration, was asked to leave a Virginia restaurant, it unleashed a gale of criticism and calls for civility in political life. There was nothing particularly uncivil about the restaurant's request – Sanders and her party were even comped on their appetizers – but naturally the backlash was swift, nasty, and notably uncivil. Then, in the way these things always go, the calls for civility were rudely rejected by activists and advocates as smiling cover for the interests of The Man, politeness as a justice-denying deference.

Politeness and civility are quite distinct concepts, of course, but that is hard to argue when the temperature of exchange is so high.[18] Perhaps the sad conclusion of our own moment is that what was once considered a declension from the norm – the norm being rational discourse of a more or less well-intentioned sort – is now the new normal, namely of presumptively ideological speech that all too often resembles the sort of madness that cannot be reasoned with. If this is so, or even partially accurate, then new lines of argument may be necessary, such as ones that operate negatively, attempting to show not why civility is a good thing but, rather, why incivility is self-defeating. This sort of collective action problem argument will no doubt appear cynical to those of a more ideal persuasion; and they may risk a certain kind of self-envelopment, giving away the stakes in search of victory, as for example when we attempt to defend the value of humanistic education with reference to its ability to secure law-school admission or a higher median income at forty years of age.

CONVICTION ADDICTION and THE SCAFFOLDS OF REASON

The murderous Nazi hate-fest in Charlottesville during the summer of 2017, in addition to revealing the extreme moral vacuity of the current White House, prompted a call for more compassion and empathy when dealing with basic ideological differences. Pundits orated on National Public Radio about how to recognize the psychological damage of those given to right-wing rage. Classes were offered in tactics for engaging those on "the other side" of political debates. These efforts and sentiments are noble but doomed to fail. Even a minute of exposure to the views of Richard Spencer or David Duke – let alone the Twitter feed of POTUS 45 – is enough to show that there is no rational engagement possible here. There is a moral baseline that Nazism is indefensible; we ought likewise to recognize, as the creators and potential beneficiaries of public discourse, that most people cannot actually be reasoned with effectively all that often. The unforced force of the better argument – to employ the standard Habermasian language – is forever butting up against actual arguments, revealed as philosophical chimera. To chastise ourselves and others for failing to ascend to the lofty plane of the ideal speech situation, or to imagine that publicity is a magic wand to heal conflictual politics, is to indulge what Jodi Dean has called the "habermasochism of media self-cannibalization."[19] No, the tactics of critical intervention must shift.

That is why, much as it pains me to say so as someone theoretically committed to the rule of reason, what we need in public debate is decisively not more efforts to understand. The utopia of a rational public sphere is an illusion, and exhortations to unearth it – in the form of core American values, Canadian tolerance, or some other political chimera – fool's errands. What we need, instead, is what social scientists call scaffolding. The term indicates measures such as air traffic control, highway roundabouts, exit signage, and queueing conventions – small mechanisms that allow humans to coordinate action when their individual interests might otherwise generate chaos. In more subtle cases, as mentioned with respect to temptations of screen time, we might seek to constrain our own desires in the form of computer apps that lock out social media access (the American Enabler-in-Chief could use one of these). Interface-specific anti-addiction scaffolds might include strict schedules of media fasting, meditation and exercise regimes, and techniques for shifting neoliberal boredom, with its in-built tendencies to send us after endless stimulus, towards philosophical reflection. In extreme cases, of course, we even impose limits on freedom for those suffering harmful physical addictions. Addicts can always try therapy or self-control, but we know that denying access to the drug or even inflicting benign behavioural modification is far more effective. All of this counts as scaffolding for addiction. Of course, at the very same time, the Interface is *itself* a form of scaffolding, since it nudges – or perhaps shoves – human behaviour in particular directions, especially those that reinforce the capitalist interests of those companies that dominate the media-sphere. Scaffolding is never neutral, but it may be erected for very different purposes: creating more profitable markets and beliefs to sustain them is just as viable an outcome as more socially and personally beneficial action.

On this point, why don't we acknowledge that political belief is also an aspect of human behaviour in need of external control? Let's call it *conviction addiction*. Such addiction bears similarity to substance-abuse afflictions, but of course is much more analogous to the addictive aspects of media use. Indeed, the two often go hand in hand, since a certain kind of platform, notably Twitter in our own moment, both allows and encourages the expression of firm, even outrageous views. The form is deliberately brief, almost telegraphic; you must make your "argument" and get out fast, discouraging any vestigial tendency to nuance or subtlety and encouraging strong, fervent language. How else, after all, are you going to generate the likes and re-tweets on which the platform trades? The Interface element here should be obvious: the user, gulled by the feeling that expressing a strong view is a form of discursive participation, has multiple incentives to ratchet up the views expressed. This ratcheting is in turn encouraged by both specific responses and the general sense of an ongoing argument. Conviction becomes its own drug. Yes, some people can, like social drinkers, moderate their views and stay clear-headed over the course of the day. Others fall into a pattern of abusive behaviour and acting out. They can't help themselves. The gateway drugs are interrupting, raising your voice over objections, and deliberately misunderstanding interlocutors – all standard moves of a CNN segment, in an instant obliterating any useful ethics of interpretation, even if there are agreed facts in play. Conviction-addicts then move on to ranting at hidden forces, demonizing ethnic groups, and sounding dog-whistles – all standard moves of Rebel Media or Sean Hannity. Finally, if unchecked, they order the fashy haircut, don the white polo shirt, and fire up a tiki torch. The fact that a slogan like "Jews will not replace us" literally *makes no sense* is, at this point, not a defect but a mark in its favour.

Classical liberals argue that bad speech should be met with more and better speech, that the marketplace of ideas will short bad stocks and return investment on good ones. Alas, not so. The mental market is far more irrational than the one governing wealth, which veers from high to low, based on rumour, wisps of policy change, and random tweets. Thus the need for market regulation, anti-trust legislation, and the Securities Exchange Commission. These are hard-floor scaffolds on trading, meant to combat excesses at the margins. Consider, then, that individual consciousness is considerably less sane than even the most rapacious corporation. Mere existence is sufficient for each of us to form a limited company in the world of thought. That's frightening! There is no dialectic possible here. Haters gonna hate.

Research indicates, as we might expect in the post-truth condition, that facts, even amply demonstrated ones, have very little pull when it comes to our states of belief.[20] This is distressing to those committed to the idea of rational mind-changing, but it is only practical to accept the limitations of reason if we are not to commit, yet again, a performative error of self-delusion. It is no rap against reason as such to note that the degree to which it operates in human thought and action is limited. It follows that appeals to reason, especially on the level of firmly held belief (of which political belief is a prominent subset), are going to be very minimal in their power. There may be some agreeable souls who, shaken by some philosophical intervention in a debate or university classroom, find some of their core beliefs begin to crumble. This is wonderful, awe-inspiring, fearsome, and of course extremely rare. Does it happen? Yes, and any teacher feels the heavy weight of responsibility associated with such scenes. It is, after all, sometimes as easy to be a charlatan of reason as it is to be its devoted midwife. Socrates was reckoned a divine presence by some, but a sly sleight-of-hand artist by others.

So let us likewise recognize the conviction-addictive quality in all of us, and stop imagining that free public discourse will bend towards reason without regulation and other forms of discursive limit. Curbs on speech and strict rules of engagement – no interruptions, no slogans, no talking points – may be the right answer in some settings. Governments already, in Canada and elsewhere, ban hateful speech. Let's go further and insist on participant-accepted discourse norms, penalties on unhelpful public outrage, and aggressively regulated social media. We could even ban media panel discussions! (This is probably not going to happen, though this proves to be a popular suggestion to those on both the Left and the Right whenever it is suggested.) On these terms, we would still co-exist, versions of Kant's notional "republic of devils" ruled by uneasy self-interest. But it will not be through talking things over, let alone hugging them out, that we maintain our modus vivendi. Limit indulgence in the cup of conviction; let's have more constraint, less conversation. When we can't agree on facts, or truth, we can perhaps at least agree on wanting to stick around and pursue our different life-plans. That's your path to a stable future, friends – by not trying to be friends.

To be sure, many people find these gently proposed measures altogether too draconian and suspect. After publishing a brief argument in favour of them I endured a predictably violent online reaction-storm.[21] I was called "next-level Orwellian," "totalitarian," a "leftist jackass" who had mastered "the political philosophy of the militant left" and offered "a pep rally to the anarchist Left." (The last correspondent was a little confused about the political philosophy of the militant Left, suggesting I move to a communist country if I didn't like it here – something no self-respecting anarchist would do. Read your Bakunin, dear frenemies![22]) Not coincidentally, these judgments came in tweets, blogs, Reddit posts, unsolicited emails, and an email letter to the editor, respectively. On the longstanding advice of the editor who published the remarks in favour of conviction-addict scaffolds, I never look at the hundreds of comments posted on the website where this argument was published, so I have no idea what went on there. That, as we all must accept, is nobody's idea of rational discourse. My favourite single comment, though, sent to my public university email, was this: "You are a moron and fake professor. Your place is in North Korea. You are a shame to Humanity." Another faithful correspondent suggested China as my proper home, which I suppose is no more (or less) appropriate.[23]

For the sake of those still-sane people who think an argument in favour of scaffolding is tantamount to an abandonment of discourse – when it is of course no such thing – allow me to expand the argument along the following rational lines. First, the abandonment of empathetic identification as the salve of public reason is not an endorsement of government coercion, censorship, "official" discourse, or other bugbears of the so-called Free Speech Movement – which is in fact code for the new Right. Witness, for example, the dismal spectacle of "Free Speech Week" at the University of California, Berkeley, which an off-world observer might imagine as a celebration of that great institution's history of liberal dissent. But no: the week was boycotted by a number of professors and many students, most of them of colour. They argued that it would prove to be no more than a platform for an ideologically obvious cluster of speakers including Steven Bannon and Milo Yiannopoulos.

Meanwhile, speaking of *actual* proposed censorship, the president sent tweets in the wake of a September 2017 terrorist attack in London, first blaming Scotland Yard for not preventing it, then suggesting six minutes later that what was needed was a "tougher" tactic against "loser terrorists": "The internet is their main recruitment tool which we must cut off & use better!" As one commentator said, "Cut off the Internet? How, and for whom? Might the Constitution prohibit such action? The President didn't seem to have time to linger on such details, because after another six minutes he tweeted, 'The travel ban into the United States should be far larger, tougher and more specific – but stupidly, that would not be politically correct!'"[24] Whatever that means.

More seriously, to note limits on empathy in the public square is not to abandon genuine freedom of speech at all. Constraint is not coercion – a conceptual elision that is itself extremely dangerous. And limits on hate are not, contrary to the view of the United States Supreme Court, limits on liberty. All speech is regulated in some fashion; there is no more an Edenic condition of unfettered freedom of expression than there is a notional free market where blind forces ever execute rational economic outcomes. All markets, whether of commodities or ideas, are likewise regulated in someone's favour. My suggestion here is that the so-called marketplace of ideas – itself a highly dubious metaphor, possibly a liberal fantasy – should be regulated in favour of pragmatic coexistence, rather than chasing after an alleged rational legitimacy that is extremely unlikely to emerge even with the best intentions in the world.[25]

A word of clarification should also be entered on the systematic misuse, or misunderstanding, of the idea of empathy. This is a form of emotional identification that is, to my knowledge, literally impossible. One cannot in fact *feel the pain of another*, despite the political rhetoric of another, more charming POTUS (for the record, I mean 42, Bill Clinton). Human emotional attachment is limited by human physiognomy; we inhabit individual bodies and there is no way to overcome this fact, even in the most intimate relations between us. One can, to be sure, be pained at the pain of another, and that is a great lever of political and ethical insight. But this is, to be precise, *sympathy* rather than *empathy*. It is what Hume and Adam Smith wisely identified as the linchpin of society, even when our individual interests are so strong that sometimes we might (as

Hume memorably said) view the destruction of half the world as of little moment compared to the pricking of our own little finger. This position, as Hume wryly accepted, is not at all "against reason," given the monstrous narcissism of most humans. Hume and Smith were realists: they, like Hobbes, took humans as they are and laws as they might be.

The main point must never be lost. Reason is extremely limited and contingent when it comes to fellow-feeling. Moreover, such fellow-feeling as does obtain is likewise extremely limited and contingent. Measuring it is probably impossible, despite the many psychological experiments that try to do so; at the same time, empathy deficits are clear enough in practice, when people retreat into self-interested, even narcissistic bubbles of their own privilege – something which, notoriously, screens tend to enable, especially among the young. Further, those who view sympathy as somehow lesser than, and maybe suspect compared to, norms of empathy should check their privilege. Furthermore, some current "empathy mechanisms," such as Facebook's "Reactions" function, whereby emojis can be assigned to posts, cannot conceivably serve any legitimate end. The Reaction function is in fact no more than another stooge for management, and it is not paranoid to suggest that the main point of the exercise – reducing empathetic reaction to clicks – is trolling for psychometric user data.

The resulting linguistic-conceptual confusion concerning empathy is, I believe, a function of generalized therapeutic culture, which imagines that emotional identification is possible and desirable, and views the merely sympathetic attitude as somehow too detached and inadequate.[26] The hard fact is that sympathy is awfully good going when it comes to human-on-human interaction. Empathy is revealed, by contrast, as a shadow-figure, a political non-starter. One senses a deep-seated problem here, where seeking some imagined empathetic connection makes the perfect the enemy of the good.

In addition, there is nothing in these modest scaffolding proposals that defies reason or even devalues its power when traction is possible. I'm all for rational changing of minds! And of course there are other uses of conversation besides rational conversion: creating intimacy, expanding one's own personal narrative, exchanging gossip, all the discursive analogues of simian or feline grooming in fact. But, contrary to Enlightenment conviction, there is no bright line between reason and its lack – we are far too cognitively complex for that to be so. Yes, rational persuasion is possible, as are moments of genuinely motive self-reflection prompted by an incisive interlocutor (the last presumptively ourselves, of course). But it is extremely unlikely that humans will achieve these ends in any reliable fashion, and almost equally unlikely that we will change our own minds – something we might have thought easier, or at least more within our control, than changing the minds of others. Once more, the hard fact is that minds do not, as a rule, tend towards change.[27] Assuming otherwise is supremely arrogant, not morally righteous, and is correctly viewed as one of the recurrent vices of the oblivious intellectual elite.

I can add, from vast and mostly unpleasant personal experience among the supposedly rational high reaches of academic life, that there is very little solace available to the pro-reason crowd. Even here, where argument is rated extremely highly, and consistency and non-contradiction valued to a degree unknown in general discussion, any possible rational meeting of minds vanishes like so much morning mist. Sad but true. The exchanges are in fact dominated by ego, social and professional position, assumed gender markers, ageism, and a host of other factors that cannot be squared with – though, yes, sometimes mitigated by – reason as such. Critics of my notion of discursive constraint should be a little less sanguine about the practical prospects of generalized rationality as a guide to real-world conversation. Never going to happen.

Third, then, it must be emphasized that there is nothing in what I propose here that favours any ideological commitment over any other one. The argument in favour of speech-scaffolds and, a fortiori, Interface limits is only valid if its telos is more robust and more productive public discourse. How would such scaffold be set in place? Some measures might emerge organically through self-regulation, though this is always a fragile prospect. Others, like universal health insurance and traffic laws, would need government backing. Even here, however, self-interest would ideally be leveraged, such that (as in traffic conventions) formal enforcement of the limits would be marginal and compliance mostly voluntary. Though critics may try to discern some larger strategy of social control in having any regulations at all on online activity and other forms of currently chaotic speech, in fact the proposal is liberal in the classical sense. That is: think just what you like, but cooperate for the general peace, such that others may do the same. The view accepts that there may be no generally acceptable social beliefs, not even somewhat vague formulations such as "common decency" (a favourite offering) and certainly not inherently controversial foundations such as a benevolent divine creator (a minority but still popular view). We should also recall that the current frontier of social-media exchange is one created and owned by private corporations. Their product is you, their customers are the advertisers who want your data. Social media like to pretend they are a public good, a discursive commons, when they are anything but that. If this is not an obvious case for regulation, I don't know what is.

Many critics suggest that there is much more possible in the way of mind-change than I allow here. People are, after all, susceptible to the force of argument, and if we are persuasive enough, they can be made to see the light. But this smacks of old-fashioned intellectual superiority, together with a large dollop of condescension: I perceive that your political views are offensive to me; I surmise that they arise from bad, or false, or ugly foundational beliefs. These can be changed! Allow me to put you into my program of discursive therapy, whereby our well-meaning, empathetic, and compassionate critiques of your basic world view will break down the base (both senses) structure of your mind. Eventually you will emerge a better and more tolerant person!

Say what you will about scaffolding as social control or "coercion," it in fact takes far more seriously the independence of persons and their minds than this program of mind control, and does not stoop to smugness when it comes to differences in political belief. Acknowledging that I cannot change your mind and more importantly *do not wish to* should be reckoned a compliment, not an insult. That an entailment of this lack of epistemological ambition is that I do not care what you believe, and have no special wish to understand why you do so, is merely the consequence of democracy. Nobody ever said, did they, that I have to *understand* and *empathize with* those with whom I am made to live side-by-side? That, surely, is asking far too much of us. When one can sometimes barely understand a roommate or a spouse of many years, supposing more with respect to random fellow citizens must be reckoned bizarre.

And so, finally, scaffolding is just that: external guidelines that help us cooperate and coexist as we pursue our various, and probably incompatible, individual projects. This is entirely consistent with my own earlier defences of civility, for example, as a virtue of public life.[28] In early versions of that defence I leaned on the Aristotelian notion of virtue as *disposition to act* and followed the central arguments of the *Nicomachean Ethics* in emphasizing imitation and habituation as the key aspects of cultivating socially positive character traits. This remains valid as a goal, but one must perforce recognize the limits of virtue-cultivation just as one acknowledges the limits of reason. We need other, more Hobbesian arguments in favour of civility to make the entire program run. Hence the identification of incivility as a collective action problem, with attendant self-interested reasons for avoiding it at the margins; and hence, too, the current argument in favour of external mechanisms of discursive sense. Civility can be expressed as rules, but they are rules in the sense of those we might accept as we enter a game-space, prepared to play fairly and honestly.

There are limits here, too, of course. Regulation can be expensive, and it can always be gamed by someone without sufficient motivation and enough brain power to figure out a workaround tactic. I am fairly certain, despite my own desires, that political panel shows and Twitter are not going anywhere fast, nor are the other addictive mechanisms of the Interface. But to introduce the notion of scaffolding, whatever form it may take, is really a reminder that we cannot continue to maintain the fiction of the empathetic citizen motivated by sweet reason.

It strikes me, in sum, that reaction to proposals concerning discursive scaffolding are themselves almost invariably ideological, sometimes hilariously so. They are rooted in the convictions of the respondents, who see only what their blinkers allow. People who wish to find state coercion everywhere read the notion of "constraint" as inevitably statist, even though this does not follow – the queueing convention, for example, requires no state and no law. Likewise for those who fear encroachment of regulation and the endgame (already noticed by Plato) that laws begetting laws is a recipe for paralysis, if not disaster. But no such program is proposed here: most relevant kinds of discursive constraint would be self-imposed. And the alleged threats to free speech are *bêtes noires* roused from slumber through selective misreading and deliberate excision of context, all masquerading as rational engagement. Ironically, these are among the very tactics that my position is meant to combat.[29]

Indeed, we can observe a series of typical contradictions in the attempted expressions of free-speech absolutism in the post-truth world. On the one hand, the views perceived to be under threat are typically labelled "unpopular," the targets of "political correctness." On the other hand, these same views are celebrated for being what *the majority of people actually believe*. Namely, strict gender binarism, free-market true belief, pro-police, and the like. If these views are indeed majority, surely they require no special protection. If they are not majority, they still deserve the same protections in law as other minority beliefs – but only on a liberal-democratic conception of the state, which is free to criticize them, even limit them if hateful or harmful. A local unpopularity, say on liberal university campuses, should surely be no more of an issue here than local unpopularity of ugly (but legally protected) views at a dinner party or community gathering. Free speech does not mean, and never has meant, the freedom to say anything at all without consequence.

Even rights regimes explicitly protecting speech do not offer the blanket protections some people imagine. The First Amendment of the United States Constitution does not apply, for example, to private companies or private universities, who may constrain speech in quite dramatic ways – as long as they are willing to shoulder the reputational consequences of doing so.[30] Individualism, meanwhile, and rights attached thereto are lauded, but individual decisions to favour more collective, progressive, or socialist agendas are dismissed as juvenile, impaired, infantilized, and so on.

By the same tortured logic of grievance, the free expression of ideas is celebrated as basic and sacrosanct, *even as* expression of criticism of specific policies and actions is routinely met by personal insults, ad hominem attacks, and sarcasm. Instead of engaging the ideas, the status of the idea-holder is challenged: "fake professor," "pseudo-philosopher," "charlatan," "pretentious," "superannuated cultural Marxist," and of course much, much worse. In a world where facts were respected, being an actual professor of philosophy, no matter what one's political views (for the record, not a Marxist, cultural or otherwise), ought to dismiss catcalls about fakery or pseudo-whatever. About pretentiousness – well, surely in the eye of the beholder. In any case, such slurs are the cries of those who cannot meet ideas with ideas but reflexively resort to personal attack. Whither the marketplace metaphors now, one wonders?

Let us accept a modestly pessimistic view on the chances of all this changing much any time soon. No single person, not even the current US president, is responsible for such widespread confusion and irrational entanglements. We have a situation in which people utter what they know to be untrue (or should) *even as* other people pretend to take it seriously as truth claims *even as* the same people in some important sense don't believe it because *even as* their failure to believe suits their political purposes and sense of outrage. The question then becomes, what can reason offer here?

The advantages of the scaffolding proposal should now be more obvious than ever. Not least is its principled combination of optative rationalism (we assume our fellow citizens are rational enough to see the benefits of a scaffolded system) and pragmatic realism (we don't presume that they are, or need be, more rational than that). There is no assumption of superiority in moral or political views implied here, which must be a better understanding of freedom of speech than mere open-season licensing. And the deep presumption that social cohesion is a goal both reasonable and viable suggests a modesty with respect to changing minds that is respectful as well as realistic concerning the prospect of agreement about what is or is not the case.

This is, in short, appropriately revamped liberalism for the post-truth era. Perhaps we might call it neo-neoliberalism.[31]

REASON WITHIN REASON

Traditional scientific method might be considered, with some justice, the ideal form of discursive scaffolding. In addition to providing essential curbs on bias and prejudice – falsifiability, reiterability, strict disinterest – the method also acts as a gate for participants. If you do not accept the rules of the game, you are not a valid player in the game. If you attempt to fabricate studies or twist the rules, you (and your results) will be expelled from the game. You can't game the rules of this game, nor can you trump them, because any attempt to do so is an automatic disqualification in essence if not in (short-term) effect. There is no possible transactional corruption: you can't buy your way to validity, nor can you overpower the game with sheer force of wealth.

In other forms of discourse, all of these depredations are possible. It is, as it were, always an open chance that someone losing at the Monopoly game of public discourse will attempt to overwhelm opponents with real-world money rather than the conventional money that operates within the game. There are, further, no clear gates in public discourse: anyone can play who wants to. This is of course a huge positive, and yet just as surely invites false trading, cheating, parasitic undermining, and all the other familiar pathogens of the public square. Most dangerously – and this is, after all, how we got here in the first place – there are precious few external constraints on such discourse. Factual claims and logical validity possess normative power, yes, but it is tenuous and variable at best, dangerously misleading at worst.

Now, it is easy to oversell this contrast. We know that scientific discourse is, like all human undertakings, shot through with social and psychological forces that mitigate against "pure" rational results. We know, too, that there is enduring disagreement within scientific subspecialties, something we might expect not to see if the results are as method-driven as we sometimes desire. This is simply the nature of complexity in discursive practices, of course. There are no such disputes in logic; there are considerably more in law, and even more in, say, literary criticism or art theory. Good interpretation becomes the essential goal, not knock-down correctness. Naturally, what counts as "good" in the realm of interpretation will itself be a matter open to interpretation. This is the best we can hope for, and it is a great deal. But even this multiplicity of dispute requires, at a minimum, some measure of good faith as interlocutors come together to compare and argue.

This last criterion of discourse in the public square can no longer be assumed – if it ever really could be. Social and technological factors have only worsened a problem that is as old as human society itself, and found in everything from large-scale politics to the tiniest domestic dispute or argument between siblings. Scientific study of our rational practices holds the key to understanding why.

Two findings stand out here. The first, drawn from a series of studies at Stanford University, provide evidence for the claim made above that facts do not have clear motive power in mind-change. In several deceptive experiments, subjects were asked to make judgments – about firefighter competence, for example – and then later shown factual claims, which they accepted as valid, overturning their initial judgments. And yet, the subjects were tenacious in their hold on *what they now knew* to be faulty judgments. This may be viewed as a version of the familiar notion of confirmation bias, but is more clearly operative than just the pleasure we get from having our prior judgments confirmed. (Other studies show that a definite endorphin boost occurs in human brains when our cherished notions are "proved right.") In these cases, the bias was in favour of judgments without confirmation. Psychologists prefer the term *myside bias* for this apparently hard-wired tendency to surrender any judgment, however erroneous, once it is made.

The second relevant scientific claim concerns the nature of rationality itself. Though we valorize it as the highest part of ourselves – a scaling of the psychic economy with us at least since Plato, indeed the foundation of the Western philosophical tradition – in fact our rational faculties are somewhat low-minded. Not only is reasoning affected by emotional, psychological, and physiological forces that have no basis in rules of inference or validity, but rationality itself is also revealed as a kind of drug. Developed during the intense socialization periods of our species, when cooperation emerged as a social good, our rational faculties are good at problem-solving and distribution of labour. But they are also inordinately biased towards winning, as in outsmarting opponents in argument or tactics.

This tendency may still fulfill cooperative needs, as when one group goes to war with another: one thinks of the myriad examples of cleverness called forth by the demands of warfare. In general, though, it means that we are very adept at spotting weaknesses in the position of interlocutors but very clumsy in seeing them in our own views. We are also forever on the lookout for breaches of cooperation within the group – free-riding, for example. This last feature, according to one tart critic, "reflects the task that reason evolved to perform, which is to prevent us from getting screwed by the other members of our group. Living in small bands of hunter-gatherers, our ancestors were primarily concerned with their social standing, and with making sure that they weren't the ones risking their lives on the hunt while others loafed around in the cave. There was little advantage in reasoning clearly, while much was to be gained from winning arguments."[32] Or, in the sharp words of a psychiatrist (Jack Gorman) and a public-health specialist (his daughter Sara Gorman), "It feels good to 'stick to our guns' even if we are wrong."[33] By the same token, two other researchers, Steven Sloman and Philip Fernbach, say, "As a rule, strong feelings about issues do not emerge from deep understanding."[34] Sloman and Fernbach's findings show, in addition, that the foundational notion of the individual rational actor, weighing options and arguments in perfect isolation and clarity, is a philosophical chimera.

So what is the solution? Some psychologists suggest that we need to be made more aware of the depths of our ignorance, especially about those things that we think we understand. The currently favoured example is the function of the common toilet, which most people can't correctly describe. Now, there is nothing disgraceful in such lack of knowledge; in fact, using tools and tricks devised by other humans, without being able to replicate or even describe them, is a perfect example of rational scaffolding. We get more things done more effectively if we don't each have to invent the crescent wrench – or the toilet, internal combustion engine, grammar, and parliamentary democracy – every single time we need them.

It ought to follow that we are individually modest in the face of this, and willing to exercise ourselves a little when it comes to the tools of human cooperation. And yet, you are far more likely to encounter someone who admits ignorance about how to galvanize rubber or distill alcohol than to do the same about the Affordable Care Act, immigration policy, comparative religion, and the working of the global economy. More humility and more study will always prove chastening to our convictions.

But how likely is that? Regulation is scaffolding that works when self-motivation and individual discipline will not. Reason itself is more a scaffold ensuring (minimal) cooperation than it is a royal road to truth. If we were to accept that, and accept further that reason works only when there are social conventions and mechanisms to prop it up, we would achieve two essential goals. First, we would see that the threats of post-truth collapse are real but remediable: reason can still win. But second, we would have appropriate wariness about the way this will happen and of the role simple expression of conviction has within the realm of reason.

We say that we should speak truth to power; but we must also acknowledge in these days how power speaks to, and limits, truth. *Reason within reason* is not a rallying cry to rival Kant's *sapere aude*, but it has two virtues that the generalized call for audacious rational self-guidance conspicuously lacks. It assumes rather than denies the social character of any rational undertaking. We are not individual heroes of reason, savvy shoppers in the marketplace of ideas. It also insists, firmly and necessarily, that reason is the only possible response to the lies, half-truth, provocations, and deceptions of the public square.

That is a conviction, not a fact. But I dare to believe it is true, and I further dare to believe that my belief will help make it so. "A great many people think they are thinking when they are merely rearranging their prejudices," William James said more than a century ago. We must all try not to be one of them.

And, just as a parting irony of this context-setting section of the text, let us note this bit of factual knowledge: this quotation, attributed to James by restless anthologist Clifton Fadiman, remains unverified. Of course it does!

PART THREE
THE CRISIS

And Nietzsche, with his theory of eternal recurrence.
He said that the life we lived we're going to live over again
the exact same way for eternity. Great. That means I'll have
to sit through the Ice Capades again. It's not worth it.
And Freud, another great pessimist. I was in analysis for
years and nothing happened. My poor analyst got so
frustrated the guy finally put in a salad bar.

Woody Allen, *Hannah and Her Sisters* (1986)

ETERNAL RETURN

How do we take seriously the recurrent theme of despair in the experience of boredom? In this section I want to pursue the question in a way that illuminates further the circumstances of contemporary boredom – that is, not just the individual's relation to specific negative experiences and the attempts, often media-based, to alleviate them, but also the structural social conditions that allow the feeling of boredom to be parsed in that way. I mean the ever-renewing mini-cycles of lurking or imminent boredom being met with, or staved off by, resort to the Interface. But more than this, there is the fact that, like all features of technological immersion, the Interface is not a neutral feature of the world. On the contrary, its alleged neutrality is part of a larger scheme of self-hiding that bears near relation to such standard forms of ideological (self-)deception as false consciousness (Marx) and cultural hegemony (Gramsci). And just as a given medium or tool is not innocent in its design-effects features, the Interface is an aspect of the human environment, the cyborg life-world, with specific tendencies. We run unnecessary metaphysical risks and label these tendencies *desires* – the Interface does not really experience wanting. But we have seen already that the complex relations underwritten by the Interface do play on, and in a way shape, our desires. Depending on the given medium, the Interface does, in a sense, "want" us to keep going on as we have been going on. It is, if you like, an *algorithm with just one salient feature*, rendered variously but always fundamentally the same, namely that we should continue to keep it alive.

That might be upsetting enough, if we could focus our attention sufficiently to reveal the Interface in its basic structure. Like the Energizer bunny, the apparent endlessness of the motion – though in fact mostly contained to a hand-held screen – borders on the uncanny, even the terrifying. In the film *Grosse Pointe Blank* (1997), a professional assassin (John Cusack) confesses to his terrified therapist (Alan Arkin) that he has a recurring nightmare about "the television mechanical rabbit," "the battery bunny." The therapist is appalled. "That sounds like a very, very depressed dream," he says.

Martin, the professional killer, wants to know why. "Martin, it's a terrible dream! It's a depressing dream to dream about that rabbit. It's got no brain, it's got no blood, it's got no *anima*! It just keeps banging on those meaningless cymbals, and going and going!" This is the Interface, in a way, but in fact worse, because despite the proclaimed power of the battery fuelling the cymbal-crashing bunny, it will eventually run down and stop. This is not so for the Facebook scroll or the swipe, because we are the batteries who provide the power, and the world is the resource that provides the raw material for the feed.

The epigraph above gives some hint of what might happen when the mechanical nature of the whole relation begins to affect the presumed anima of the human part of this particular equation. In Dee's novel *A Thousand Pardons*, the confession of crippling boredom is likewise made within the therapeutic scene when Ben, a Manhattan lawyer, and his spouse try to assess their apparently loveless marriage. She imagines that she has been providing, at some considerable cost to her own intellect and ambitions, a stable suburban domestic life for this urban breadwinner. He, meanwhile, has watched with bewildered horror as his self was consumed by the very same structures of late-capitalist life. A different man might figure that he is a victim of neoliberal norms of getting and spending, the bulldozer logic of money-making, property, and credentials. Ben has no such theoretical apparatus at his disposal; instead, he embarks on a clumsy sexual pursuit of a much younger associate. This is inconclusive in one sense – they never have sex, though she does undress for him once in a hotel room – but decisive in another. Confronted by a boyfriend he was not aware of, Ben is beaten up and later drives drunk into a roadside accident that will end his career and his marriage. So much for shaking off the bonds of boredom!

Every moment of a Woody Allen performance, meanwhile, is a kind of therapy session. In this instance, his character has just learned that some sudden hearing loss in one ear is not the result of a brain tumour – his typically paranoid assumption. Walking in the street afterward, he summons the ghosts of Nietzsche and Freud, and the memory of an actual therapeutic session, in order to highlight the cruel features of everyday life. Here is a man who can read and think! And yet, there is of course no succour here; the Eternal Return is just another way of having to be bored, not the test of *amor fati* that Nietzsche intended. Freud's pessimism, as it is styled, is revealed not as a fount of insight about the human condition but as just another in a relentless series of moments where nothing happens. The salad bar – than which there is no clearer indication of 1980s middlebrow happiness – is the desperate solution, but for the therapist, not the patient! Boredom spreads its dark wings across the entire scene, casting a shadow of ennui that holds no hint of a breakthrough, not even the confused and half-assed acting out of flirting with a co-worker twenty years younger than yourself, or drinking a bottle of vodka while tooling up the West Side Highway.

There might be another way out. In the internal monologue of the Woody Allen character, delivered in characteristic voice-over – this film in particular is full of the much-derided cinematic device – the musing continues: "Maybe the poets are right. Maybe love is the only answer." That is a nicely placed "only," since there is a forbearance here from suggesting that love is *the* answer, as in the solution. After all, surely this is a case where love is not enough. But as answers go, maybe it's better than nothing. Better, anyway, that the endless peregrinations of philosophical-therapeutic intervention, which add nothing in insight to what a poor man – or anyway, a Woody Allen type of man – might perceive without their help, or even despite it.

Well, maybe. This is a question to which we will return, if not eternally then at least once more before our time together is done.

STRUCTURAL DESPAIR

It's later now. It's always later, now. That's what our now means. In what remains of this text, and our time together, I want to focus more specifically on the complex relation between two aspects of the boredom literature, or taxonomy: on the one hand, Schopenhauer's contention that boredom paints a visage of real despair on the individual; and, on the other, Adorno's insistence that the structures of boredom are social, not merely psychological. My aim here is to sketch a landscape of *structural despair*, of which the individual experience of boredom, and the desperation to relieve it through technology, are the main symptoms – not "mere" symptoms, however, because there is in fact nothing more severely indicative than this two-step of everyday emptiness of the deep rot of the way we live now.

In the fall of 2017 I attended the Canadian Science Policy Conference in Ottawa. This is an annual wonk-fest of the sort routinely held in national capitals and conference centres around the world. The main idea is to discuss the nature of scientific research as it impinges on the realm of public policy. The attendees are much as you would expect: civil servants, NGO officers, graduate students, policy experts, and, of course, working scientists. Because the then-newish Liberal government in Ottawa had vowed to reverse the muzzling of scientists that had been implemented by the Conservative governments of Stephen Harper, a man for whom science must be some sort of clinically sealed bran-box activity with no social implications whatever, there was a sense that this iteration of the conference might offer a little muscle-flexing from the keepers of scientific results. Indeed, this anticipation was rewarded.

The newly appointed governor general of Canada, the Queen's representative as nominal head of state in Canadian parliamentary democracy, gave the keynote address. Julie Payette is a former astronaut and a prominent woman of science. She did not shirk from the opportunity to attack what she viewed as the forces of social and political ignorance with which science must struggle. In a wide-ranging speech, she attacked the deniers of climate change, creationism, the advocates of astrology, and various other purveyors of fake news and alternative facts. Payette was roundly criticized for this perceived breach of protocol – apparently many people believe that governors general and other titular office-holders should limit their activities to ribbon-cutting and cookie-rolling. God forbid they should have views and arguments – including perhaps the view that there is no God to forbid or allow anything. A minority view, of which I am an advocate, held that Payette should feel free to air her views just like any other public figure, assuming they do not actively impair her ability to execute the duties of her office. Why the hell not? (There also is no hell.)

For myself, I was part of a session on "trust and expertise in the post-truth era," which was tangentially related to this controversy precisely because of the notion of post-truth – 2016 word of the year in the *Oxford English Dictionary*, that wishful arbiter and dedicated reporter of usage – was in everyone's minds. In this session, some sad but unsurprising things were noted. For example: with the advent of social media and crossfire accusations of fake news, many traditional sources of expertise – government, the mainstream media – are now actively distrusted. Business and NGOs have lost traction. Corporate CEOs with sky-high salaries aren't trusted, but neither are academics (sad!). Meanwhile, peers matter more than strangers with credentials.

These findings, quantified in what is known as the annual Edelman Trust Barometer, offer statistical confirmation of what most of us already suspect. One finding, though, struck me as outlandish. The most trusted sector in the economy, well above food services (66 per cent), consumer goods (63 per cent), and the despised world of finance (54 per cent), is technology – trusted by 76 per cent of those polled "to do what is right."

This last result is, we must acknowledge, objectively bizarre. The self-appointed gods of Silicon Valley have made no secret of their contempt for the constraints of democracy. They may value people as potential consumers, slices of market share for the next ballyhooed product rollout, but these are individuals reduced to handy cash nodes, not bearers of rights or entities worthy of respect. Yes, the *übermenschlich* libertarians of the tech world, people like anti-suffragist Peter Thiel and master of bafflegab Tim O'Reilly, are hailed as oracles. This despite the obvious fact that their techno-utopian futurism is socially exclusive, male-dominated, and wilfully blind to its own environmental and political costs. It's a very nice world if you're on the inside, no doubt, but for the bulk of the globe's population a post-national regime of unfettered "innovation," with attendant regulatory capture and shirking of tax burdens, is a living nightmare. And it's the present, not the future.

So what accounts for the high rate of trust for these priests of the trans-human, with their promises of eternal life for the lucky few and distracting phone apps for the rest of us? It's a potent brew of wonder at what O'Reilly likes to call the "magical user experience" and a kind of aspirational luxury-logic, where we overlook labour abuses and sexual harassment because of the slick product-promises they underwrite. In fact, this mixture of stimulus and willing credulity is exactly what is captured by the notion of neoliberal boredom. Why perform due diligence on the source and costs of your chosen device or platform when it is so much easier to apply the balm of stimulation? These products are here for us, after all. Their promise is happiness and freedom from routine ennui.

One can see the appeal of tech trust, in short, the secular faith in device-enabled ease that moved people to heap flowers outside Apple stores when Steve Jobs passed into the ether. But comfort always comes at a price, and hiding the costs behind the glow of your screen does not change that reality. Technology is more an environment than an economic sector, as omnipresent and comprehensive as the air. To paraphrase Obi-Wan Kenobi circa 1977, it surrounds us and penetrates us. Unlike the Force, however, it is executed mostly in proprietary formats that demand constant upgrade, plus media platforms and search engines that look public but are in fact private corporations with hungry shareholders to feed.

But wait, you say: the toys! the toys! This is Candyland in your hand! Who doesn't love that? Quite a few people, actually, though they tend to be ignored because they are the disenchanted and the disenfranchised. They realize that the apparent democratization of social media invites false consciousness, while the liberations of phone-extended consciousness enable soft slavery. You don't have to be a Luddite to think that, so far from trusting the purveyors of our everyday zombiehood, we should be subjecting them to the sharpest possible criticism. One might even be tempted to bite the bullet and simply be a neo-Luddite, ideally with the realization that this is an option only for the lucky and blessed. The sly ensorcellments of Silicon Valley conceal cynical realities of oppression and entitlement. It's a long con that could do with some debunking. In an earlier moment of the tech revolution, actual visionaries like Neal Stephenson and William Gibson demonstrated what an unevenly distributed future looks like. Poverty and suffering are not illusions or glitches in the system; they are part of its intrinsic logic. Government and media may be imperfect, but at least they claim to be in the service of the *demos*. The tinpot deities of tech don't even do that. Why do we give them the time of day, let alone our money and our loyalty? Trust me, resistance is not futile. Better yet, trust yourself.

The relevance of this issue to the current study should be obvious from what was expounded in part 1, but let me offer a specific and recent example to drive the point home. The tech sector are at once the dispensers and defenders of the Interface; they depend upon our own addictive attachments for their livelihood and their outsized delusions of grandeur. If the market for screen products did not exist and were not so reliably subject to renewal in the form of upgrade anxiety, there would be no pooling of wealth in the sector, and hence no tendencies to look beyond national borders for the equally reliable resting places for that wealth. The self-aggrandizement and guru status follow as emergent properties of wealth-conferred status: the familiar cycle of advantage in one respect underwriting, however spectrally and invalidly, a claim of advantage somewhere else. This is a variant on the usual forms of excessive entitlement disorder, whereby family wealth (say) seems magically to confer on its beneficiaries a sense that their political or (gah!) aesthetic views are worthy of special respect. The tricky part of earned rather than inherited wealth is that it tends to obscure the market basis of its generation – people who make things believe that their claim to the benefits thereof are more intrinsically owned than those who simply find themselves on third base as a matter of birth and yet think they hit a triple. The Ayn Rand version of privilege is that, if you really did hit the triple, all the benefits are yours by natural right. Except that there are no rewards if there are no customers to pony up. Absent the eyeballs and finger-swipes, the inventions mean nothing.

This is why the basis of Interface economies is not the devices, or even the desires that fuel them. This despite the advertising and product-rollout narratives that emphasize features and efficiencies, as if the new phone models were akin to new models of Maserati or Rolex. In fact, the analogy to other high-end goods is false. A luxury item, if material, can advertise only one thing: itself. (More specifically, it advertises you as someone who is able to afford that good.) An Interface-driven good can pretend not to aspire to luxury status, and hence apparently democratize both prize and appeal, because its hidden engine is potentially limitless: which is to say, all the advertising that the platform can bear and – even more significantly – all the customer data that the platform can deliver to other parties.

The obvious case in point is Facebook, the behemoth of social media. Its story is too well known to require any detailed elaboration here, recounted in *The Social Network* (2010), as irritating a film as one can imagine, and then ingested wholesale into popular lore. We all know by now how the site evolved from a collegiate dating-aid to a multi-billion-dollar online newsfeed, friend nexus, and global communication device. To be fair, the real-life Zuckerberg seems far less odious, though also far more cartoon-like, than the Jesse Eisenberg caricature of the film. (Though he did say, in 2018, that he would not take down Holocaust-denying posts from the site "because I think there are things that different people get wrong" – a conception of free speech that many critics found all too loose.[1]) After the 2012 initial public offering of the company, artfully delayed to enhance value and interest, the company's value expanded to US$500 billion and showed no signs of lagging – until there was a significant glitch when it was revealed that Facebook had partnered with British data-mining firm Cambridge Analytica to use the data of eighty-seven million Facebook users for election influencing. The company's ballooning early value might seem hard to credit, given that the platform is available for nothing, until we recall what in fact inflates that balloon, namely the revenue poured into the company by other outfits looking to capitalize on its awe-inspiring ability to gather personal data from its customers. Quite apart from Facebook's despicable complicity with Russian interference in the 2016 US presidential elections, its spectacular indifference to the rights and interests of its dedicated – in fact addicted – users is nothing short of breathtaking. This apparently innocuous news source and networking device is in reality one of the most pernicious features of a political structure that uses human boredom as a lever to maximize profit and undermine democracy. The company suffered heavy stock losses in July 2018 when trading erased 23 per cent of its revenue in two hours, at an estimated value of some US$120 billion – the biggest one-day tumble in its history.[2] Was the bubble finally about to burst?

Well, until that happens, let's consider the reality of everyday Facebook use, which is an especially toxic kind of dependency. Sadly, most users don't care much about the election scandals – even though they know that, at the very same time, the company doesn't care much about them. Sandy Parakilas, a former platform developer for the company, worked on Facebook privacy issues in advance of the IPO. "What I saw from the inside was a company that prioritized data collection from its users over protecting them from abuse," Parakilas wrote in 2017.[3] "Facebook knows what you look like, your location, who your friends are, your interests, if you're in a relationship or not, and what other pages you look at on the web." This aggregation of data, supplied to advertisers, allows for targeting of more than one billion Facebook users every day. Worse, because there is no external oversight of this situation and currently no external regulation of its near-monopoly on this information, the company experiences no incentives to reverse its instinctive market-drive value ordering and protect its customers. "Facebook is free to do almost whatever it wants with your personal information," Parakilas continued, "and has no reason to put safeguards in place." And indeed, by the latter part of the new century's second decade, calls for a Facebook "constitution" were becoming less fanciful. The site "has a philosophical, institutional allergy to making qualitative judgments about truth and falsehood," tech writer Max Read argued, even as "it's become something that resembles a state when you squint at it – it holds near-supreme power over media and civic attention."[4] This unfettered sovereignty either has to be made into something more like a liberal democracy, with rules and regulations to benefit users, or nationalized under an existing liberal-democratic nation-state. A third, scarier option would be for Facebook to enshrine its status as a state power in an explicit way, making users into "citizens" – or, in reality, force-fed chattels.[5] "Would a Facebook constitution 'solve' the Infowars problem?" Read wondered. "A good one that balanced the competing needs of the public sphere, individual freedom, and civic health, and that gave people a voice in and an understanding of the decisions being made by the platform, might at least get us as close as it's possible to come."

And until *that* happens, the answer is still government regulation. But in capitalist markets, regulations need to be experienced as real costs. There is no other way to incentivize compliance in anything like a consistent way. Even with stiff regulation there looms the prospect of regulatory distortions, in which, say, lobbying and selective litigating costs are reckoned to be lower than compliance costs. Meanwhile, the platform continues to operate in the same manner, trading attention and personal information for advertising revenue. One feature that Parakilas singled out for special opprobrium was the series of "addictive games" whose "free use" was in fact purchased at the price of granting the game-development company free access to players' personal data. "Unfortunately for the users of these games, there were no protections around the data they were passing through Facebook to outside developers. Once data went to the developer of a game, there was not much Facebook could do about misuse." This might include using the harvested data to develop profiles of children without their consent, or using a game to solicit all of your photos and messages, even though these were irrelevant to the game or app itself. Parakilas notes that efforts to investigate such cases were deflected, and any negative stories about the practice squelched.

At this point one is tempted to see this as a nightmarish science-fiction scenario, in which some highly addictive game is used as cover for a program of alien mind control. (The *Star Trek: The Next Generation* reboot includes just such a storyline.) But the aliens here are just your friends and neighbours, operating within standard market parameters. Their mind-control efforts free-ride on our tendencies toward, and fear of, being bored: to call a game "highly addictive" is, after all, just another way of saying that it repeatedly, but only temporarily, staves off the sense of *not* being occupied and stimulated. This is the hard core of neoliberal boredom, that its promise is one of alleviation of the very symptom, which it then acts to induce and extend. And all with our willing, indeed enthusiastic, participation.

The Russian manipulation of Facebook reached an estimated 126 million American voters (or potential ones, if they tore themselves away long enough). That is an obvious international violation of sovereignty that happened entirely because the platform, and its attendant Interface, is not regulated. The routine commercial abuses of personal sovereignty are just as challenging to a functioning democracy, but they do not arouse nearly as much appropriate ire. This is (Parakilas again) "a company that reaches most of the country every day and has the most detailed set of personal data ever assembled, but has no incentive to prevent abuses." Conclusion: it must be aggressively regulated, or its monopoly on data broken up. Whatever you think about the reality of prospects for this, it does not go nearly far enough. Facebook is Exhibit A in a networked system of Interface influence. It uses our desires and fears against us. This is no mere metaphysical critique, whereby we might miss deeper philosophical insight in our rush to keep the game going or the feed scrolling; this is the production and consumption of selfhood being actively abetted by the political and economic system as such – the current arrangement, for lack of a better phrase – in which many participate blithely, glibly, happily. Don't blame the advertisers; they are just following the logic of the system. No, we have seen the enemy, and it is us.

But wait: we do, don't we, want to keep the focus on the structural aspects of everyday despair? Recall a point from part 1, that blaming the victim is not a productive argumentative or even rhetorical strategy when it comes to cycles of addictive desire. But neither is it the case that all regulation is good regulation, or all scaffolding in the interests of its subjects. We can invoke here the notion of *nudging* and the debates it has generated in policy and public circles alike.

We all know that the Nobel Prize for economics, like its subject, runs on controversy. You won't find here the heated debates about whether Bob Dylan is really a writer, but many laureates – *New York Times* columnist Paul Krugman is one – arouse as much ire as admiration. Economists are like medieval theologians, coming to mental blows over how many angels can dance on the head of a pin. The 2017 winner, the University of Chicago's Richard Thaler, is a case in point. With colleague Cass Sunstein, a prolific jurist and former White House "regulation czar," he popularized the notion of "choice architecture," otherwise known as *nudge*. In a series of books they argued that government has a responsibility to create mechanisms by which citizens will make better choices.

The motivation here is already obvious: whether from boredom, laziness, or sheer stupidity, we humans are not very good choosers, even when it comes to our own welfare. For example, many people, through inattention or confusion, make bad decisions about their retirement savings. So there should be mandatory plan contributions, with opt-out clauses. Likewise organ-donation schemes for drivers, which ought to operate in reverse of the current norm: you must actively choose not to donate. More mundane examples include the everyday hilarities of cellphone auto-correct, or a measure directed at people who overload and overeat in fast-food restaurants. Eliminate trays in these eateries and you will cut down on both waste and waistlines. Everybody wins!

Nudging is not always about making things better for bodies and the body politic, of course. Those supersize-me offers at a burger chain, or the up-rigged pricing of soft drinks at the movies, are examples of choice architecture too. So are credit cards, negative-billing plans for utilities, and cable-channel bundling. Critics find the very idea of pro-welfarist nudging paternalistic, and indeed the view has come to be called "libertarian paternalism." This is government regulation over what many people consider a basic political freedom, the ability to choose whatever the hell I want, including things that might be bad for me – and maybe the world.

There is no such thing as an unstructured choice, of course, any more than there are unregulated markets. The question is always, who benefits from the given architecture or scheme of regulation. Thaler and Sunstein think good architecture means greater welfare for everyone, and when they sail close to old-fashioned Big State elitism, as when they suggest more sophisticated choosers should help out those less savvy, they can always fall back on opt-out clauses.

But it's not that simple. A more searching critique of "nudge-world," as the political philosopher Jeremy Waldron has called it, is that it compromises autonomy and dignity, not just simply freedom of choice. Even when we know that choices are structured, whether by well-meaning state agencies or rapacious marketing companies, like the ones who opposed the so-called Big Gulp ban on oversized soft drinks, we still feel that the experience of freedom is basic to selfhood. (Recent findings suggest that the stricture on soft-drink portions has had no discernible public-health effect.)[6]

On this view, we are diminished when we are guided, like rats, toward the good welfare cheese in the social maze. Nudging is a subtle version of the charge that afflicts all utilitarian social arrangements, namely, that they don't show respects for persons. That's a good point, and yet the central problem remains. We need external structures to make things function, not only because we are often irrational choosers but because we are often actively bad people. Insisting on unfettered choice is like saying we should all be playing bumper cars at the carnival when what we really need are speed limits and traffic laws. This strikes me as a pretty good metaphor for current "debates" about free speech.

So resent them as much as we like, nudges aren't going anywhere. They are as old as barter and as tricky as statistics or three-card monte. The pathos here belongs to the human condition itself. Maybe we should aspire to be better choosers, but it's so much work. Why not let some wonk's choice architecture do the thinking for me, as long as I *feel* free? In the end, nudging highlights our internal tangles concerning desire about desire. We might wish we were better, more autonomous and dignified selves; but maybe not today. Today, choice architects, I just want to fill my tray!

Social media and the web more generally might be viewed as the mother ship of all fast-food emporiums. Not only do you get a tray, you get one after the other, filled as high as you like. The parallel positions quickly emerge: some consider this the height of freedom of choice; others see it as imprisonment by other (self-imposed) means. The debate about net neutrality provides a useful focus for the issue as it relates to our present concerns about agency, addiction, and the self.

In the late fall of 2017, as part of the Trump administration's legislative agenda, a proposal to roll back net neutrality was set to go before the US Congress. The relevant background is this: since its inception, the Federal Communications Commission held to the position that all internet content, and all providers of it, are equal – or, at least, that they walk on an even playing field. Internet service providers are not allowed to discriminate between sources, even if it would be very profitable for them to do so. If they could, selective pricing or two-tier service would inevitably emerge, with some powerful content providers – you can easily imagine who they might be – given faster and more reliable routes to customers. Small providers, outliers, perhaps politically marginal groups, would be shunted into a slow lane or maybe even denied service altogether. They would technically exist on the web but would not be able to reach the eyes of potential audiences.

Now, the FCC – chaired since 2013 by former wireless and cable lobbyist Tom Wheeler – has decided to abandon neutrality and pursue sweeping changes to the provision of internet content. The issue is exacerbated by the fact that most people are strictly limited in their choice of provider. As of late 2017, the four big cable companies – Comcast, Verizon, AT&T, and Charter – accounted for 76 per cent of the 94.5 million internet subscribers in the United States. Some 96 per cent of customers had two or fewer (which is to say, one) choices when selecting an ISP. Territories have been split among these companies in various non-compete agreements that may violate antitrust legislation, and create what amounts to a shared monopoly and forms of price-fixing. These companies thus have both sides of the potential transaction covered: they can dictate what content consumers see, and they can demand higher fees from the companies who wish to engage those same customers. Even in merely market-based terms, this is a serious failure. In larger political terms, depending on how you view the potential and place of the web, it may also entail a democratic failure.

For critics, revoking net neutrality is tantamount to an authoritarian crushing of free speech. Here is political commentator Sarah Kendzior on the stakes in the era of President 45 and his relentless projects of social disruption:

> For nearly a year, America has stood at the crossroads of a damaged democracy and a burgeoning autocracy. If net neutrality is destroyed, we will cross firmly into the latter, and our return is unlikely. The threat to net neutrality highlights the reliance on social media and an independent press for political organizing in the digital age. Should net neutrality be eliminated, those avenues will likely become curtailed for much of the public or driven out of business due to loss of revenue. Without the means to freely communicate online, citizens will be far less able to challenge the administration.[7]

Well, possibly. Certainly, if you accept Kendzior's basic premises – that the internet is essential to political resistance, and that is why the current regime wants to limit it – then very bad things must seem to follow. Less spectacular, and perhaps more likely, is that a non-neutral net would widen existing digital divides, making it harder for certain sectors of the population (rural dwellers, for example) to view the same cornucopia of choices that flood the screens of more privileged citizens, and also harder for them to sell things at a distance. Sludging, not nudging.

That is an equity argument, but not necessarily an argument about democracy. Is the net really that obviously a democratic good? With all respect to the kinds of grassroots action that Kendzior and others are engaged in, calling out untruths and doing basic research about gerrymandering and state-sanctioned disenfranchisement – "The repeal of net neutrality will stem the flow of information, making voter suppression harder to document," she insisted – there are two immediate objections. First, that kind of information-flow is at best a tiny sliver of what the net does, and a vanishingly small slice of its content, drowned in the floods of falsehood, misinformation, and hatred, not to mention pornography, silly memes, and sheer triviality. Second, the net is not in fact a necessary condition of conducting such efforts at political resistance. Old-fashioned media still make most if not all of that political action possible. Even communication and organizing, two features of political resistance repeatedly cited as benefits of the web, are entirely possible without screens, let alone with a two-lane internet. Would-be activists might have to leave their offices a bit more to make it happen, but maybe that's a good thing.

Behind these two is a third point, which is not quite an objection so much as it is a conclusion driven by a different premise. The internet is not in fact a public good: it is not and never has been, in the jargon of economics, non-rival and non-excludable; there are always associated costs in either accessing or influencing it. It is at best a highly structured and regulated communications medium that supports a variety of private enterprises, some of which are for profit and some not. On that basis, it is far from clear that it is an un-alloyed good for democracy, unless we mean by that the unfettered desire-extravaganzas imagined, and deplored, by Socrates in Plato's *Republic*. Equal access to markets and equal status for all desires is not what democracy means, or anyway should mean.

Only an unthinking commitment to choice of any kind, in short, and freedom of expression for everything imaginable would make one conflate democracy, as an ideal of legitimation, to mere unrestricted choice. This is a common error, especially in the neoliberal age, where consumer choice is far more of a daily reality than deciding on a political mandate – and where the latter becomes, too often, itself a matter of consumer choice. But even more, if choice is never not structured, and it is not, then equally expression is never free – there are always constraints and interests in play, regulations and thresholds past which even avowed absolutists will not go. Indeed, as we saw earlier, it has become a caricature of the so-called alt-right that they invoke free-speech absolutism – unless and until it comes to those who dare to criticize them. Objections to their hateful views are then construed paradoxically as censorship (how so, when it's not the state objecting?), suppression of diversity (again how, when there is no mechanism for this?), or a matter of "politically correct" ideological indoctrination (once more, how, when the free exchange of *all* information is supposed to be the highest neoliberal good?).

The question, as always, is *cui bono* – who benefits? Of course, like many people who have spent hours on "help" lines or waiting for a technician to arrive sometime between noon and 6 p.m., I feel almost instinctively that anything a cable company wants is probably something I don't want. (These concerns, by the way, are the signal exception when it comes to tech trust: polled respondents have lower approval rates for Comcast and Verizon than for Bank of America, General Motors, or Taco Bell.) It's also the case that Comcast et al. have made no secret of their desires for the rollback, investing some US$4 million in lobbying the FCC and Congress between 2014 and the first part of 2017, and a whopping US$18.8 million in 2013, second only to defence contractor Northrop Grumman. These efforts, which went unreported by Comcast's news divisions (NBC, CNBC, and MSNBC), can only be in the service of future potential profit, cloaking base motives in dry legislative "reform." As one critic put it, ironically given our present concerns, "The cable companies have figured out the great truth of America. If you want to do something evil, put it inside something boring. Apple could include the entire text of *Mein Kampf* inside the iTunes user agreement and you just go agree, agree, agree, what, agree, agree."[8]

Meanwhile, these coordinated threats to net neutrality have made strange political bedfellows of grassroots activists and large providers such as Netflix, Facebook, Google, and Amazon. One is fearful of losing what feels like access; the other is fearful of losing potential customers. But these providers already significantly influence how we entertain ourselves, how we interact with each other, how we know things, and how we shop. I'm not really too worried about their interests, since among other things we know that they will be able to pay whatever it costs to get fast-lane access. Or, as one mealy-mouthed telecom lawyer put it, "hyperspeed lane" access, since everyone else will already be in the fast lane. Nice try, my friend. Two tiers are two tiers, even if one of them is defended as better than nothing.

Government regulation of tech giants, meanwhile, has been slow to emerge or absent altogether. Part of this hesitancy or outright hostility when it comes to regulatory measure is obviously linked to deeper background ideologies and political commitments. In July 2018 the European Commission, administrative arm of the European Union, levied an unprecedented US$5 billion fine on Google for breaching the EU's rules for market competition. Google's Android operating system is used by an estimated 85 per cent of the world's cellphones. Google was using its bulldozer influence to force cellphone manufacturers to pre-install the search engine, as well as its Chrome web browser, violating the interests of customers and competitors alike. "In this way, Google has used Android as a vehicle to cement the dominance of its search engine," said Margrethe Vestager, the EU's competition commissioner. Vestager went on, as her job title might suggest, to justify the fine mainly in terms of blocked competition and innovation, but we can spare a thought for the hapless phone users forced to confront Google and Chrome whether they liked it or not – and then probably using them anyway, since what could be easier? The EU has also been much more aggressive than the United States in data protection and privacy: its 2016 General Data Protection Regulation aligns issues of explicit consent and the right to know who has access to data with general legal measures to protect human rights. Facebook, for example, estimated that about a million users had fallen out of its clutches as a result of the regulation.

The EU's bold regulatory move against Google predictably called out an enraged Twitter rant from Donald Trump, then engaged in the first actions of a protracted and nasty trade war with Europe, China, Canada, Mexico, and pretty much everybody outside American borders except Russia. "I told you so!" he wrote, in characteristic style. "The European Union just slapped a Five Billion Dollar fine on one of our great companies, Google. They truly have taken advantage of the US, but not for long!" There is a history here, of European regulations levying stiff fines on American tech companies. The European Commission had previously fined Google US$2.7 billion after it determined that the search engine favoured its own shopping tool over those used by rival online companies. (Google challenged the first fine and intends to appeal the second as well.) Politicians from both Republican and Democratic parties, including former president Barack Obama, have argued that Europe is seeking financial benefit from a sector in which its companies can't adequately compete. "But the argument that the EU is going after US companies for self-interested reasons doesn't match the facts," wrote political observer John Cassidy. "It would be more accurate to say that successive Administrations in Washington have deliberately overlooked mounting evidence that the large US tech firms have abused their monopoly power, and that the victims of these alleged abuses, including many American companies, have been forced to take their grievances across the Atlantic."[9] Attempts at regulation closer to home have been mostly blocked. In 2012 staff members at the US Federal Trade Commission concluded, in a 165-page internal report, that Google's conduct had "resulted – and will result – in real harm to consumers and to innovation in the online search and advertising markets." They recommended an anti-trust suit against Google for its restrictive contracts and forced bundling of apps.[10] But in January 2013 the five commissioners of the FTC, all political appointees, overruled their own staff and voted 5–0 not to pursue any legal action against Google.

The Interface is not the technology; it is all the facets of social and political influence that make technology possible in our attention economy. As so often, the users of the technology are the real losers, all the more so when attention is usually fixed on rival companies who share the same agenda as the giants but lack the market share to back up monopolistic ambitions. The users are chided for their laziness in using market-dominant tools that are extremely difficult to bypass. Or they are chastised for not resisting the dominant companies' plans more boldly, by deleting accounts or going on self-imposed media fasts. But when the options are structured as all or nothing – the sly logic of the bundle or tie-in, where the only lasting solution would seem to be not having a phone or a computer at all – users can't win for losing. In these market-based cost-benefit analyses, poor everyday users are somehow *always already wrong*.

ENDLESS AND IMPOSSIBLE JOURNEY

But blaming the addict, however popular and apparently in-eradicable a pastime, is entirely out of place when it comes to the Interface. As Michael Schulson has pointed out, comparing online addiction to gambling, "Overwhelmingly, the academic literature on gambling has focussed on the minds and behaviours of addicts themselves. [Yet] there's something in between the gambler and the game – a particular human-machine interaction, the terms of which have been deliberately engineered."[11] Moreover, as Natasha Schüll notes in her 2012 book *Addiction by Design*, that interaction has been structured by hundreds of very clever people whose main goal is to capture and hold your attention – even as we keep blaming you, the individual, for surrendering to it.[12] Schüll's focus is electronic slot machines in Las Vegas, a particularly virulent form of addictive machine, but her insights about the deliberate design choices that make for addiction are valid across a range of examples. She also emphasizes the network of choices made by designers, users, owners, and enablers that make gambling addiction so hard to shake, as well as the mostly hidden gender and class disparities observable in slot-machine addiction.

We keep getting it wrong with respect to what is happening in such addiction, however. One review of her book carried the rhetorical headline "Can Objects Be Evil?"[13] Well, they can enable and encourage evil effects, certainly. But they're probably not evil in themselves (what would it mean for them to be so, any more than a drug is?). The language surrounding technology can itself have a responsibility-nullifying effect, not just in the implicit ideology of inevitability about "progress" but also in subtler tics that let us off the hook when it comes to the machines and software we use. We speak in terms of compulsion, not choices; we use force language rather than agent language. Linguist Maggie Balistreri, author of the witty *Evasion-English Dictionary*, makes the central point turn on a simple choice of verb: "Technology doesn't *make* me do anything, it *lets* me do anything," she writes. "It enables me to see someone face-to-face and it spares me from seeing someone face-to-face. It lets me connect or avoid."[14]

Even the addiction language, which retains elements of the metaphorical (not every hard-core screen user is physically dependent), can enable a wry evasion of the behaviour in question. "What you get sucked into is not the one thing that caught your attention – your text message or tweet or whatever," Carolina Milanesi, analyst at the technology research firm Creative Strategies, is quoted as saying to Farhad Manjoo, the prophet of Peak Screen noted earlier. Instead, Manjoo writes, "You unlock your phone and instantly, almost unconsciously, descend into the irresistible splendors of the digital world – emerging thirty minutes later, stupefied and dazed." Milanesi agrees: "You open this irresistible box, and you can't fight it."[15] People tend to laugh self-deprecatingly when they speak of their addictive tendencies concerning ever-present smartphones, something that only the singularly depraved would do if the stimulus in question were instead gambling, alcohol, or drugs.

So is it the designers who are the real devils in play? Well, yes and no. In one sense, following the usual imperatives of rational interest, they are simply selling their cleverness for money. So it's the owners? Yes, but not entirely. And so on – except that one consistent fact is that the users themselves are almost always in line for disapproval. Indeed, in almost every case it is the users who shoulder the blame for their addiction, and the designer and owner – usually anonymous, absent, or too big to fight – who are assigned half-hearted and ineffectual demonization. "In short, it's not exactly a fair fight," Schulson writes. "When you read enough articles about internet compulsion and distraction, you start to notice a strange pattern. Writers work themselves into a righteous fury about prevalence and potency of addict-like behaviours. They compare tech companies to casino owners and other proprietors of regulated industries. And then, at the peak of their rage, they suggest it's the users – not the designers – who should change."[16]

Neil Levy, in discussing addiction as a failure of extended agency, notes tellingly that individual selves have limits in their ability to exercise control over wayward desires. "Unified selves are a result, at least an important part, of negotiation, bargaining, and strong-arm tactics employed by subpersonal mechanisms as they attempt to achieve their ends," he writes, echoing the notion of mind divided against itself that is at least as old as Plato.[17] Of course, as any addict knows, one can become habituated to all the twists and turns of one's own tactics – the subtle postponements, the bargaining, the false promises and broken oaths. This, in fact, is what addiction feels like; that is why the psychology of addiction is so consistent across such different classes of stimuli (drugs, alcohol, tobacco, food, gambling, sexual promiscuity, work, violence, etc. etc.). And so, in a more Aristotelian twist, these tactics are understood to be environmental as well as individual. "Addicts are too fragmented for normal attention-distraction techniques to have much chance of succeeding; instead they are most successful when they structure their environments so that the cues which remind them of their drugs are entirely absent."[18] Such structuring raises the opportunity-cost of the drug, via isolation or medication that induces a negative reaction; or it changes their relationship to their desire-driven discount curves, offering rewards for time spent abstaining, or regular fellowship meetings in which to celebrate abstention. But the limits on these tactics is obvious to anyone who has dealt with a genuine addict.

Bolstering such mechanisms with more obvious extra-personal environmental controls offers the possible fallback line of defence. Price regulation, criminal levies for possession, bans on use in certain times or places, family/peer pressure, and organized social disapproval are all effective measures to curb addiction. We could add here such things as suicide fences on known sites, entailing a pause for reflection that is often sufficient to deter the suicidal person, or advertising campaigns that heighten awareness of unplanned harms. These external mechanisms, like the curbs on speech discussed in the previous section, all constitute forms of scaffolding. Agent-harmful desires are not obliterated but, rather, rendered excessively costly – if only temporarily – so that the urge to satisfy is overpowered. By the same token, de-scaffolding conditions that offer easy access to stimuli, especially when combined with other factors that compromise full autonomy, such as poverty, family dysfunction, or genetic predisposition, make self-control that much more difficult to execute. (Note that some mechanisms, particularly family/peer pressure, are ambidextrous in this regard.)

Levy may still be too individualistic in his view, however. "Self-government, like political government, requires a monopoly on the coercive powers of the agent."[19] But perhaps this is not so; after all, the achievement of a flourishing self, with will extended over time, might be counted as a public good. We want fully (if not ideally) autonomous agents for all kinds of familiar social reasons: to be good citizens, good parents, productive members of the cultural sphere, and so on. Surely there is a stake in structuring the social environment that goes beyond coercive self-control, as powerful as that can be under ideal conditions.[20] This extension beyond isolated individual desires and actions is, indeed, the presumed rationale of "sin taxes" and substance-control regulations of all kinds. Would such mechanisms not be appropriate to the forms of autonomy-impairment associated with the Interface, even if we hold off the conclusion that such immersion is a case of full-blown addiction?

Shulson believes so, at least tentatively. He advocates greater control over a user's experience of the Interface, especially when it comes to the basic experience: regulating notifications and advertising, for example. More radically, perhaps there is a case for banning certain features of "compulsive design," such as Facebook's endless scroll or the dating apps' swipe function. In addition, heavy or obviously compulsive users of certain Interfaces are easily identifiable using existing preference-monitoring algorithms. There could be triggers that "time out" users, post alerts, or cut off access to given sites. Such mechanisms are already available on the self-control side of the ledger, blocking access to social media according to a previously posted limit. This is, in effect, a use of extended agency to reinforce a weaker self from the (prior) position of a stronger one. Perhaps some Interfaces themselves demand such a feature as a condition of access. More radical regulation is also possible, for instance by limiting all forms of access according to set times and central controls. These would be highly unpopular, of course, but we should note that virtually everything we know as feeding harmful desire is regulated in some such agent-external function, from outright criminality to liquor licensing and limited opening hours. Even foodstuffs must now carry labels indicating the precise breakdown of their ingredients.

The other obvious route of improvement in this quarter is the rise of "ethical design." If we stop blaming users for their engagement with various Interfaces, yet maintain that such engagement is harmful, it follows that designers – like purveyors of drugs, fast food, prescription pharmaceuticals, or gambling venues – have certain special responsibilities. These might include, first of all, a sense that design ethics is a concern separate from profit margin or responsiveness to shareholders – that, indeed, social media and other forms of technological scenes are public goods.[21] More concretely, Joe Edelman has argued that we can use the traditional insights of economic choice theory to demonstrate that many of the (designed) choices on social media are harmful ones, "regrettable and isolating," in his words.

These harms can be addressed by more conscious menu design, allowing for greater freedom of choice – and hence possible goods that do not threaten autonomy – even as a public database of menus, choices, and outcomes could be compiled to track the evidence. (One current limiting feature of these debates is that most of the "evidence" amounts to anecdotal accounts, usually framed in unhelpful pro-or-con terms.) Such a database would put on record the hidden costs and false promises that are all too common among existing Interface designs, allowing us to judge their alignment – or otherwise – with our informed and beneficial desires.[22]

There is, to be sure, a rival view, specifically on the issue of boredom and happiness. Many urban designers hold the conviction – often but not always unexamined – that boredom is always bad for those who experience it. In an effort to minimize stress, they advocate eliminating the occasions for boredom in, say, a street or park. Lack of interesting sights or stimuli pushes the brain into a condition of stress, such that individuals in the condition are more likely to engage in risky behaviour to eliminate it. Thus, in a tricky extension of the neoliberal account of boredom, an argument is advanced that alleviating boredom counts as a public good, or at least an important goal in design. The assumption here is that stress is always bad, something to be eliminated as quickly as possible.

Now, far be it from me, as someone influenced by architectural theorists Rem Koolhaas and Jan Gehl,[23] to advocate *against* better street design; but there are some large gaps in the line drawn from principles of good design to a general program of constant stimulus. Gehl, for example, following the classical thinking, argues for variety, not stimulus; this must include, crucially, those periods or stretches of the landscape in which we are under-stimulated, even bored by being so, such that our thoughts may process the stimulus experienced before and savour the potential renewal of stimulus at some future point. And while nobody would argue in favour of needless suffering, there is a danger, I think, in viewing all affect-negative experiences as ones to be avoided at all costs. Sometimes being under-stimulated is a good thing in and of itself. (This is distinct, I think, from the religious understanding of boredom as a frustrated under-employment of one's powers of thought and action – what Erich Fromm called a "paralysis of our productive powers."[24])

The design writer Colin Ellard has marked out a connection with addictive behaviour of just the sort discussed earlier. "Researchers discovered that even brief boring episodes increased levels of cortisol, which fits well with other recent suggestions that there could actually be a relationship between boredom and mortality rates," he writes. "Boredom can also lead to risky behaviour. Surveys among people with addictions, including substance and gambling addictions, suggest that their levels of boredom are generally higher, and that episodes of boredom are one of the most common predictors of relapse or risky behaviour."[25]

Ellard concludes with a sort of half-concession concerning boredom. "When the external world fails to engage our attention, we can turn inward and focus on inner, mental landscapes. Boredom, it has sometimes been argued, leads us toward creativity as we use our native wit and intelligence to hack dull environments," he notes. "But streetscapes and buildings that ignore our need for sensory variety cut against the grain of ancient evolutionary impulses for novelty and will likely not lead to comfort, happiness or optimal functionality for future human populations." And, lest you be wondering, yes, there is an app for that: properly equipped, your phone can tell you when you are bored – just in case it was not obvious to you. According to the MIT *Technology Review*, "A group of researchers say they've developed an algorithm that can suss out [your level of boredom] by looking at your mobile activity, considering factors like the time since you last had a call or text, the time of day, and how intensely you're using the phone."[26]

There is even a partial solution for those who experience the twitchiness of missing their phones during those times they are unable to have it in their hands. The analogy to smoking is obvious: how many addictive behaviours are related to the seemingly simple, yet actually complex, phenomenological question of *what to do with my hands*. When someone becomes conscious of an almost physical need to handle the phone, a strange but common psychosomatic dependency, a therapeutic intervention might seem warranted or even desired by the sufferer conscious of his or her own enslavement. Enter the Substitute Phone, an invention of Austrian designer Klemens Schillinger. This helpful "device," according to reports, "comes in five models and reportedly looks and feels like a standard phone."[27] But "instead of a screen there are stone beads embedded in slots at a variety of angles. The beads allow users to swipe, pinch and scroll in order to satisfy the urge of pulling out your smartphone." These fantastic objects, our age's version of Greek worry beads or (maybe better) a suckling child's "dummy," "pacifier," or "binkie," are fashioned from black polyoxymethylene that feels like a working smartphone, with beads made of Howlith stone to simulate the swipe and scroll functions of actual phones. Designer Schillinger argues that "the Substitute Phone aims to calm users and helps them cope with the withdrawal symptoms, also called the 'checking behaviour.'" There is hope for the hopelessly addicted, at least in the form of a dummy! But alas, this object – so essential to the moment – is not widely available, leaving observers with the suspicion that the design is more artwork than therapeutic aid.

In any event, with this looping of dependency and its related tropes, including therapy for the addictions we develop, the neo-liberal argument has come full circle. Boredom is induced by an environment; it is experienced by an individual as stress; the stress must be relieved; addictive behaviour is a possible version of the cycles of relief. Worst of all, this is evolutionarily hard-wired into us! Therefore we must do everything we can to limit boredom in the first place. But let us call out the social and political assumptions in play more clearly. Novelty in itself may answer some parts of our hard-wiring, but it is not in itself a good. Moreover, boredom can be experienced under any circumstances, sometimes especially those where there is a great deal of stimulation and easy, short-term satisfaction of desire. Boredom is the symptom, not the disease. To assume otherwise is merely to fall prey, once again, to the neoliberal account of the self.

No doubt the debates on these points will continue. Let us simply remember that behind all such efforts, and the political arguments about them, lies the issue of the globally autonomous self, something we must continue to view with a skeptical eye. Not coincidentally, there is a Kafka resonance here. The late novelist David Foster Wallace, discussing the peculiar character of Kafka's humour, noted how hard it was for him to convey the comical quality of such apparently dark works to his American students. The problem, Wallace said, was that Kafka's humour did not fit any of the obvious categories that the students already had in hand. It was not satirical, or ironic, or slapstick, or sentimental.[28]

It was, instead, something deep and forbidding, yet altogether familiar because human. In Kafka we meet ourselves, as if through a glass darkly. Josef K, accused and convicted of crimes neither he nor we understand, helps his hapless executioners figure out how to wield the knife that will end his life. The man before the apparently locked door to heaven, in his derangement, begins conversing with the fleas in the collar of his tormentor's coat (the door has been unlocked the whole time). The humour here, Wallace argues, is not something you "get," the way you get a joke. His students are baffled because "we've taught them to see humour as something you get – the same way we've taught them that a self is something you just have."

No wonder, then, that they cannot appreciate the essential Kafka joke, a species of irony at once comic and tragic: "that the horrific struggle to establish a human self results in a self whose humanity is inseparable from that horrific struggle. That our endless and impossible journey toward home is in fact our home."

Precisely! We will not confront this fact and thus never appreciate the complexity of achieving selfhood *at all*, let alone effortlessly, as a mere presupposition, if we are forever in the condition so vividly described by T.S. Eliot in "Burnt Norton": "Neither plenitude nor vacancy. Only a flicker / Over the strained time-ridden faces / Distracted from distraction by distraction / Filled with fancies and empty of meaning." Insofar as we concentrate on banishing boredom, or sublimating it into creativity or further consumption, we merely postpone – perhaps indefinitely – a confrontation with self that is essential to self. An endless and impossible journey may well be often boring. Nevertheless, it is the journey upon which all of us are embarked.

SELF-CONSUMPTION

Technology is an environment, as surely so as air or the natural realm. Indeed, a central feature of our existence now is that there is no natural – as distinct from artificial – sphere of reality. What we call the natural is thoroughly conditioned by the human-formed realities of the Anthropocene. This will be obvious to some, controversial to others. But consider how long this has been coming, and how many voices have joined in the chorus of its remarking. The cliché has it that Turner invented the sunset, decisively conditioning our experience of a daily astronomical event with the layers of mediation that make it impossible to see a setting sun in anything except a manner layered with meanings visual and otherwise (romance, mortality, nostalgia). More to the point, for present purposes, is Heidegger's reminder that technology is not a tool or set of them, not even an attitude, but instead a way of construing the world as a whole. In the form of *Ge-stell*, or enframing, technology reveals its world-making powers, the manner in which it makes everything available and potentially disposable. In a blunt example, the "standing reserve" of the forest is shown forth as potential lumber, the waterfall as potential hydroelectric power.

But we should never imagine that the enframing effect, the re-situating of the world as standing reserve, does not include ourselves. We too are resources, to be produced and consumed as elements of the larger disposability. We are commodities for work, as in "human resources," those workplace environments that claim to protect us under the unwitting sign of commodification. More seriously, we are consumables for our own desires and pleasures, the way the very idea of "self" becomes a kind of product that might be ingested in the same way as a video game or Netflix video. Indeed, we might even aspire to the level of "coherence" offered by such classically narrated products, given that our own selfhood existences often lack the structure associated with commercial products. We wish we could be as curated as something produced with a multi-million-dollar budget for a bored audience scrolling through the streaming possibilities.

There are ramifying effects of this self-consumption. The Interface is the mechanism by which they operate and dominate. We are self-consuming when we are swiping and scrolling, subverting our consciousness to the platform in search of connection or illumination. We are self-consuming when we surrender to the mundane temptations of the timeless present, the present of shopping or surfing, which has no past and no real future. Recent warnings about the lures of "presentism" are, appropriately, put in appropriate historical context by recalling Debord's analysis of capitalist time in *Society of the Spectacle*. Or, perhaps even better, we can recall the dire language of Virilio, perhaps the most insightful philosopher of technology and time: "This is brilliant. Contraction in time, the disappearance of the territorial space, after that of the fortified city and armoury, leads to a situation in which the notions of 'before' and 'after' designate only the future and the past in a form of war that causes the 'present' to disappear in the instantaneousness of decision."[29]

Under such conditions, the Interface is a timeless drug, an endless addiction with no relation to real past and real future, let alone what we might still venture to call actual purpose. Consider a fictional speculation that bears on the point. In Annalee Newitz's 2018 SF novel *Autonomous*, a rogue drug developer has released a pirated version of a drug meant to enhance productivity.[30] This is in response to the global corporate influence of a pharma multinational called Zaxy, whose new landmark drug is Zacuity. "Zacuity is reducing the number of dopamine receptors on the neurons in the midbrain and prefrontal cortex," a character explains. "Doing this interferes with decision-making, and makes the brain extremely vulnerable to addiction. As he loses more and more of those receptors, he gets more addicted to the specific thing he did while taking the drug." The patent-pirate notes the corporate-capitalist stakes here. "That's good news for corporations who licence the drug from Zaxy," he points out, "because you've suddenly got a bunch of workers who are obsessed with going to work and completing projects."[31]

But the pirate's knock-off version of Zacuity turns out to be mortally addictive. People become obsessed with painting walls, or making doughnuts, or executing decisions in a transit system – even, in one catastrophic example, "regulating" the systems that keep New York City from drowning under a deluge of subterranean Atlantic Ocean wash. They don't die from the drug itself, but rather from secondary effects like dehydration and immunity depletion. They are working so hard and so much that they literally cannot take care of themselves. These are workaholics gone wild, with psychochemical boosting. The remorseful drug pirate tries to halt these effects, with the aid of a rogue free lab of genetic designers and reverse engineers, by in effect creating memory deficits that will break the cycle of addiction. If the Zacuity-addled subjects can be made to forget the cycles of dopamine excitation that cause the cascading effects of work-unto-death, they might survive, even at the cost of some short-term memory loss.

Unfortunately, and ironically, this renders them useless as workers if the version of the drug they ingested was the corporate version rather than the more benign knock-off. "Suddenly the Quick Build workers wanted to go bicycling, play with their kids, watch videos or develop software for personal projects," we are told. Meanwhile, the withdrawal effects were literally nauseating. "The pirated Zacuity users recovered quickly, but corporate users suddenly found themselves with months of memories that made no sense. They were unable to bounce back. Maybe they would never be able to do their jobs again without throwing up."[32]

One can read this less as speculative fiction and more as a wry commentary on our tortured relations to technology and devotion to work, perhaps the most obvious emergent property of capitalism's everything-is-commodifiable inner logic. Task-specificity is the goal of all technology, and our consumption of self via this imperative is even more comprehensive, it seems to me, than the leisure and pleasure memes favoured by other purveyors of the speculative nightmare. "I'm making *decisions!*" wails one victim of the Zacuity addiction, even as she sends subway trains crashing into each other. The feeling of purpose is stronger than the feeling of mere pleasure, and – to use somewhat dramatic language – the Interface *knows* this. The Interface thrives on decisions, even if they are empty, addictive, or harmful. That is the essence of its relation to boredom. We are never bored when we are making decisions – or painting, or baking doughnuts, or whatever Zacuity makes us want to do, endlessly. By contrast, as we can visualize in our own lives but also in related near-future speculations such as the endless cruise-ship of life that features in WALL-E (2008), we may well become bored when we are experiencing nothing but pleasure.

Experience suggests that we consume the self in numerous potential ways, not excluding nausea. My suggestion here is that we do so most thoroughly in the form of (what we imagine is) purpose.

Because this is relationship – between self and what it believes, and as always as facilitated by technology – is so basic to everyday life, it can be difficult to appreciate the extent to which these conditions are enabled by ordinary technological conditions. Likewise, it can be difficult to imagine what political and personal resources we can muster in the face of what seem like inevitable realities.

But of course, as usual, the most insidious aspect of technological ideology is precisely the idea that the depredations we isolate are inevitable. Heidegger hints at this essential point, even as later thinkers – Ellul, McLuhan – make it more evident. But eternal vigilance is the price of individual freedom in the world ruled by the Interface. Nothing is natural until we make it so, nothing is inevitable unless we accept it as such.

PART FOUR
WAYS OF GOING ON

MOOD REPORT
gnostic,
ironic,
reflective,
dreamy

Your true traveller finds boredom rather agreeable than painful. It is the symbol of his liberty – his excessive freedom. He accepts his boredom, when it comes, not merely philosophically, but almost with pleasure.

Aldous Huxley, *On the Margin* (1923)

And so, for the time being, a question familiar from all experience of crossroads, at least before the advent of Google Maps and dashboard GPS systems: where do we go from here? To begin an answer let us, again like old-fashioned map readers, trace the path of where we have been.

The subject of boredom keeps shifting its registers and modalities along with cultural and especially technological circumstance. The most profound philosophers of boredom – Schopenhauer, Kierkegaard, Heidegger, as we have explored already – strove to chart its terrain for eternal metaphysical verities. Others denied the validity of these existential accounts, or emphasized instead the psychic and evolutionary and creative uses of boredom. But the plain truth is that boredom is a condition inextricable from particular circumstances and the way they are structured in relation to human consciousness. Boredom doesn't merely happen; sometimes it is deliberately created. There may *be* common features in the experience of boredom itself, the restlessness and "wish for a desire" that Tolstoy and Adam Phillips identified; but we cannot estimate boredom's force accurately without also bearing witness to social and political context. The advocates of technological solutions to technological problems always tout the wider benefits of their new tools. What if wider social benefit is a potential already within us, waiting to be released?

Boredom has often been associated with the expanded leisure time and individualism of the modern era, and that is true as far as it goes – though we should note once again some of boredom's more ancient forebears such as acedia, or *accidie*, "the noonday devil" of inaction and lack of interest in all things that was said to afflict cloistered monks. This "sorrow of the world," as Thomas Aquinas called it, involved a state of listlessness about things that relates to both modern-day depression and the cognate sin of sloth. It was considered a failure of duty to the divine gift, possibly a step on the fatal road to suicide, that affront to the Holy Spirit itself. A modern inheritor of this tradition, Jean-Charles Nault, takes up the cudgels for Thomistic-Aristotelian virtue as pitted against the evils of modernity and our recurrent acedia. "Although the midday sun comes to bathe everything in its dazzling light, acedia, like an obscure malady, plunges the heart of the person that it afflicts into the gray fog of weariness and the night of despair," Nault writes. "Acedia endures. It is not a short-lived crisis. It is a radical, chronic evil [that] causes a stifling of the intellect, the *nous*, whose function is precisely to contemplate God."[1] The only reliable route out of this chronic condition is virtuous action, the purposeful and excellent performance of one's proper identity. "Remember that Saint Thomas presented moral action as being directed toward a goal," Nault enjoins us. "This goal is what gives action its meaning, its sense, so that this action can become an anticipation of beatitude and a preparation for it. From this perspective, acedia appears as the temptation to make *nonsense* out of the moral life. Thus the profoundly immoral character of this vice becomes evident: acedia admits that absurdity might be the last word in human life."[2]

Absurdity may indeed be the last word in human life, but absurdity properly conceived is not incompatible with action – quite the contrary. Secular boredom of the more recent past is, as we have seen, at once more common and less serious. "Boredom, hopelessness and despair have always existed, and have been felt as poignantly in the past as we feel them now," Aldous Huxley notes in an essay on how acedia has evolved into something more proximate and democratized, associated with the overstimulation of cities. "Something has happened to make these emotions respectable and avowable; they are no longer sinful, no longer regarded as the mere symptoms of disease."[3] The morality of boredom has likewise shifted. What was once an affront to God is now often considered an affliction of the childish or immature mind, rather than the vice-ridden or despairing one, the self with no ability to sustain interest in something. On the other hand, you will sometimes hear people say, in tones of pride, that they are "easily bored" – as if this were a mark of mental discernment, an unwillingness to be easily pleased, when it is probably more like a mental defect.

But to the bored person, and I assume that means almost all of us at one time or another, boredom is never a minor thing. At an extreme, say as experienced by a long-term prisoner in solitary or an infantryman on deployment, it amounts to a kind of torture. Less spectacularly, as we have seen time and again, it is mundanely dissipating and unpleasant. Boredom, whatever its degree of severity, amounts to a stall or block in the self's relation to its world. Foiling this stall or breaking open the block can feel like emerging into sunlight after a long enforced darkness. I now know what to do with myself. I can once more *act with purpose*. But because all boredom is relational in this phenomenological, self-to-world way, it can be difficult to get the account of it right. Why, exactly, do some of us find others of us boring? Why, by the same token, can the very same activity – listening to opera, fishing, watching a baseball game – count as bliss to one person and a thumbscrew to another?[4] (I want to leave open the possibility that there are objectively boring things, places, and people; but this claim seems burdened with an epistemological weight that is unnecessary. If there is no one there to be bored, is something still boring?)

Part of the latter answer resides in the tangled undergrowth of taste, that most unreliable of aesthetic and cultural concepts, as Veblen has taught us. Since there is no accounting for it, taste will not help us much here – or at least it will not help us any more than it helps anything else, including the philosophy of art or late-night discussions of pop music. It is entirely unsurprising, as Bourdieu maintains, that our preferred pastimes and stylistic commitments in dress or leisure, our entire *habitus*, should exactly match the social and cultural position that we occupy.[5] Dispute is impossible here, and this is so despite the Kantian attempt to leverage an antinomy of taste, not because we cannot access each other's experience, but rather because the structures of taste are in fact socio-cultural, not personal.

At such a point, many people would be inclined to look again to psychology for the definitive account of boredom, just as we observe mainstream discourse inclining towards psychological accounts of conditions and issues once thought to be under the purview of philosophy: evil, happiness, existential moods, and so on. And indeed there is now a vast literature on the subject in that quarter alone. The results are mostly unsurprising: boredom is a matter of intolerable levels of under-excitement; it can be "cured" through new stimulus or, sometimes, mental exercises that help avoid this and other "mind traps" such as those associated with procrastination, to which it bears close relation. (To reiterate, both are conditions in which there is a second-order desire with respect to a missing first-order desire: I *wish* I wanted to do something instead of just sitting here. I *want* to want to do my taxes, but I can't get down to it.)[6]

But however accurate and even helpful, psychological accounts of boredom always seem to miss two crucial points. The first is an old insight, articulated best by Heidegger, though also by Schopenhauer. Once again, let it be said: maybe boredom isn't something we should be *fleeing*; it might be an important symptom of a more general existential malaise that bears thinking about. After all, whatever else it does or may become, boredom signals a problem with the world and our place in it. The second point is part of a larger, wholesale critique of modern capitalist society. One can scoff at this critical ambition, of course, especially given the ideology of inevitability that surrounds neoliberal global capitalism, but we must see that contemporary boredom is not just a function of modernity but specifically of the political constructions of work and leisure. Boredom is itself, on such an analysis, a form of capitalist ideology, facilitated by the peculiar self-cancelling presuppositions of the Interface.

Once we of-the-moment phone-heads appreciate fully that boredom is driven by extra-psychological factors, factors that are beyond the purview of the individual qua individual, we can begin to see the relational, dynamic lines of influence from our screens to our states of mind. This should be obvious but is still denied, or ignored, by those who set undue store by the idea of mental self-control. Since we all have ample evidence of the weakness of the human mind, in particular of the will, when responding to mental excitement, this amounts to denial. Thus we return to the most vivid portrait of boredom from our own day, that all-too-familiar picture of someone, maybe even several people apparently sitting together, all with their eyes glued to a smartphone screen and their fingers flicking, flicking, flicking. What do they want? What do they *not* want? (The repetition of the action is here matched by my deliberate repetition of the image: how many times do we confront this scene in an average day?)

These people are not in that moment bored, or at least they would likely deny being so if asked. The point is rather that this behaviour is intended to ward off any lurking boredom, to forestall the block before it has a chance to form. There is likewise a kind of anxiety functioning here, even if the outward appearance is calm. People do not want to miss anything, or fall out of touch, or have to rely on their own internal thoughts – to say nothing of having to converse with their like-minded phone-scrolling tablemates, an unthinkable prospect. What we observe here, in short, is a quietly desperate attempt, always doomed to fail, to stave off any encounter between the self and its desires. Boredom is the invisible, because exorcised, spectre that nevertheless haunts the whole scene.

The addictive aspect lies, as argued previously, in the endless quest to find *satisfaction* from the scrolling. The Interfaces created by certain devices and platforms are specifically designed to prevent satisfaction, even while promising it. Let us face the hard truth again: Facebook's endless feed, Twitter's unrelenting chirps of messaging, the streams of texts from friends and co-workers, the email inbox that never reaches zero – these are all, philosophically speaking, versions of those feed boxes into rat experiments where an edible pellet drops with every successful push of a button. Media are like any other drug, as we have seen, even if their patterns of addiction are not simply analogous to other forms of more obviously physical dependency. Even if we are somewhat cautious about bestowing the label of drug, and of addiction, it is clear enough now that media should be treated with due respect for their harmful qualities. They are not neutral, as if there were no in-built tendencies meant to drive us to addictive behaviour. On the contrary, that is exactly what they are meant to do – and what they succeed in doing, as long as we let them. No wonder there is now a thriving counter-industry of articles and books defending silence, solitude, media vacation, and the like.[7]

Let it be said that silence, no more than studying boredom, cannot *solve* our problems with respect to desire and its tangles.

Nothing but death, the final absence of desire, can do that! But Heidegger was right that the correct attitude to boredom is one of rigorous fascination. John Cage was offering a serious motto, or manifesto, when he said, "If something is boring after two minutes, try it for four. If it is still boring, try it for eight, sixteen, thirty, and so on. Eventually one discovers that it is not boring at all but very interesting." But of course one must first overcome the basic reaction, not simply philistine but deeply and widely felt, that the artist is, in some sense, having us on, making mischief as a way of provoking thought. One recent writer on boredom judged 4′33″ as "his most famous example of this strategy," warning that this was "a big ask, and one that didn't always pan out for Cage, who remains a controversial figure in music history." But the judgment, so phrased, is banal; it makes it sound as though being *controversial* were somehow akin to being insane, or worse, incompetent of normal judgment. "How do you bore people," the critic asks, "without making them hate you?"[8] Because obviously making people hate you is a really, really bad thing to do, even for an obscure avant-garde artist! The same critic says this: "So much modern art is deliberately monochrome, slow, or repetitive – even John Baldessari's declaration 'I will not make any more boring art' is presented as a repeating line of text, over and over. *I will not make any more boring art, I will not make any more boring art, I will not make any more boring art* … more like a meta joke than a serious motto." Note to critic: yes: it is a joke! It is also a serious motto. This ironic effect is achieved by making a statement about not being boring into a boring statement. Joking and serious intent are not, after all, incompatible except in the dedicated irony-free zones that still somehow seem to persist in American culture.[9]

This kind of refusal to take boring art seriously might seem innocuous, even bracing, but in fact it is dangerous nonsense, intellectual philistinism dressed up as "common sense." Ernst Gombrich's once-canonical "Pleasures of Boredom," for example, which celebrates the aimless play of the doodle in loosening up the strictures of artistic discipline – a clear version of creative boredom – not to mention more searching interventions from the Continent, seem lost in the shuffle of a bluff Anglo-Saxon refusal to take challenging art seriously.[10] This attitude misses the force of Gombrich's insight that "delight lies somewhere between boredom and confusion," that liminal state where we perceive something of Kant's purposiveness without purpose, an incipient meaning not yet brought into clear focus.[11] To ignore the pleasure here, for both the creator and the spectator, is ultimately far worse than even the laziest pages of Alain de Botton or Malcolm Gladwell, those smiling brain-servants of the current arrangement. This is popular thinking about ideas that is really just middlebrow culture-industry product – the sort of thing, as Adorno wrote of bad Hollywood movies, where every visit to the cinema leaves you feeling "stupider, and worse."[12] Such commentary is a depressing sign of the times: so-called thought about boredom that is not only itself boring – the lurking paradox of the subject – but also replicates the worst tendencies of the Interface. In short, this is intellectual complacency masquerading as cultural analysis, no better than a TV panel discussion.

So let us be serious about boring art, art about boredom, and the place of boredom in the experience of art. There are many ways in which modern art has approached, appropriated, and deployed the condition.[13] Cage's dictum about time articulates a classical, and essential, position. He begins his larger aesthetic investigation by suggesting that the problem of boredom lies with the perceiver, not the thing perceived. In such a case, demand more and longer. This enjoinder is consistent with Cage's interest in Zen Buddhist thought, the power of the mantra or the incantation, and the penetration of ordinary perception with forms of ritual repetition and extension. He almost undermines the argument by suggesting that the perceived thing ("it") at some point ceases to be boring, but the real point is that we, the perceivers, reach a point of wisdom at which we no longer perceive it as such. We are the ones who have been changed, not it – for it, after all, is just what it always was, only over and over again. Taken in such a spirit, this is an example of what Julian Jason Haladyn calls "the will to boredom" – the principled exercise of the possibility of boredom to challenge our existing frames of meaning and sense – to put us, as Walter Benjamin had it, on "a threshold to great deeds."[14]

In her published notebooks one can find Susan Sontag meditating, in a similar vein, on the relationship between art and boredom. "People say 'it's boring,'" she notes, "as if that were a final standard of appeal, and no work of art had the right to bore us. But most of the interesting art of our time is boring. Jasper Johns is boring. Beckett is boring, Robbe-Grillet is boring. Etc. Etc."[15] One could indeed go on with such a list, from Melville to David Foster Wallace, but most striking is the highlighting of the issue of a "right to bore." Why should art be denied this right? After all, it is exercised by virtually every other human experience and product at one time or another. Even a slam-bang action movie full of explosions and "snappy" dialogue can prove boring, sometimes excruciatingly so. "Maybe art has to be boring, now," Sontag muses, without endorsing any view that suggests boring art is necessarily good art. Obviously not. But "we should not expect art to entertain or divert any more. At least, not high art. Boredom is a function of attention." Sontag goes on to expand the last point in an illuminating way for our purposes. We often find a work boring because we lack a capacity for the kind of attention it demands. Sometimes the greatest art is what teaches us how to appreciate it, just as the most demanding spectacles and pleasures might qualify as acquired tastes. We should be wary, in short, of the tendency to reject art because we find it boring, as if there was nothing else to consider. Boring art, like boredom itself considered philosophically, is an opportunity for deeper reflection.

For the record, I have never personally found a performance of 4'33" boring in the least, nor have the students for whom I regularly stage or screen these performances. (I'm not quite sure how I feel about the 4'33" app, which you can download for your iPhone then use it to record and share your own "performance" of the piece.[16]) The point is not to redeem boredom by rendering it inert through interest, but to challenge our perception that something is boring in the first place. Cage's 4'33" is not really *about* boredom. It does not deliberately invite that experience for aesthetic and philosophical purposes. Rather, its purview is time, silence, and sound – even while offering a pertinent philosophical investigation of what constitutes a musical composition or performance. The key insight about modern art and boredom comes instead, as so often, from Warhol: "I've been quoted as saying 'I like boring things.' Well, I said it and I meant it. But that doesn't mean I'm not bored by them."[17]

Many artists work this rich seam of paradox, the liking of boring things because they are boring: Martin Parr's postcards, the Situationist *dérive*, or aimless urban drift, Georges Perec setting down the tedious catalogue of things that happen on one Parisian street corner.[18] Perec's devotion to the "infraordinary," the non-event, opens up to view "what happens when nothing happens." He is particularly attentive to the comings and goings of regular city buses on the street, such that the book seems at times to resemble a schedule of their arrivals and departures – another instance, in all its trivial exactitude, of the Interface in its larger sense. The attempt to exhaust the place does not succeed. The observer himself grows bored even with his self-imposed boredom. More significantly still, there is no possible exhaustion here: a place, any random location, especially in a busy city with many circulatory energies, simply goes on and on. There is, as it were, always some nothing going on.

The Invisible Committee, irascible and hilarious nihilists, complain with dark glee about the faux-therapeutic character of contemporary culture, the failed attempts to alleviate boredom with cheerful pro-forma gestures. "All those 'How's it goings?' that we exchange give the impression of a society composed of patients taking each other's temperature," they grumble in *The Coming Insurrection*. For the Committee, boredom is endemic to modern social life because of the essential isolation and narcissism of the individuals who populate any given society, especially in the developed world; our coping mechanisms are rendered not just ineffective but ridiculous. "Sociability is now made up of a thousand little niches, a thousand little refuges where you can take shelter. Where it's always better than the bitter cold outside." Their crusade, insofar as one can claim that they have a coherent political aim, is to counter the myriad social and political forces that make every place, in Paris and everywhere else, have "the look and feel of a highway, an amusement park or a new town: pure boredom, passionless but well-ordered, empty, frozen space, where nothing moves apart from registered bodies, molecular automobiles, and ideal commodities."[19]

One might also mention in this connection the existential-noir novels of Jean-Patrick Manchette, where bourgeois boredom in post-1968 consumer culture is disrupted by sudden outbursts of criminal violence; or the novels of J.G. Ballard and Michel Houellebecq, in a later and bleaker register, which make similar arguments.[20] The films of Austrian master Michael Haneke, especially *Funny Games* (1997, remade 2007) and *Caché* (2005), skewer middle-class complacency with elements of intrusive, insistent violence and the suppression of knowledge necessary to lead a life of dull privilege. These are uncanny, oneiric, and unsettling works of art about the social relations of production and its strongest emergent property, boredom. They are anything but dull. They remind us to respect Debord's insight that the routine spectacles of late and especially postmodern capitalism are always feeding us more dissatisfaction under the sign of satisfaction. To turn away from this, to drift off, is a revolutionary act precisely because it invites a condition of reflection in the very midst of networks of sustained stimulation. We float free of the spectacle as a way of reclaiming the traces of individuality and purpose that are obliterated by the spectacle.

There remains a place for those works that are themselves enervating, making the experience of boring art its own endgame. When I wrote a book about the Empire State Building, I considered subjecting myself to a screening of Andy Warhol's 1964 film *Empire*, which consists in a single slow-motion shot of the building sustained for eight hours and five minutes.[21] I won't lie to you: I didn't watch the whole thing. This was in part because Warhol himself averred that the unwatchability of the film was part of its point. Not for me to dispute with the master about his own creation. Lists of top-ten boring films are naturally an evergreen temptation in listicle-style journalism (*Elizabethtown*, *The English Patient*, and Kevin Costner's post-apocalyptic turkeys *The Postman* and *Waterworld* often appear). But to list *Empire* with these is to commit a category mistake: the other films are intended to be entertaining, at least among other goals and however haplessly; Warhol's study of time and an urban monument defiantly is not so intended. But it is not always easy to say what a work of art wants from us. For years, every time I tried to watch Wim Wenders's acknowledged masterpiece, *Wings of Desire* (1987), I would fall asleep. No matter how caffeinated or determined, whether midday or early evening, the thing reliably sent me to the Land of Nod. Was it me, or was it the film? Is this celebrated work of art, I wondered, in fact *a very boring film*?

Here is an answer that may prove a key to all future investigation. The movie is dreamy, and so boring in just the way dreams are: revelatory and strange. Art works, sometimes just because they are boring, have the effect of plumbing the depths of what the conscious, ordered mind cannot appreciate. This is not the only thing art does, nor is it the only lesson boredom teaches. But we should always heed what makes us feel like we are losing our firm grip on the ordinary world. Call it a text message from the unconscious: TTYL! (That's SMS-speak for "Talk to you later," in case you didn't already know, though its origins lie further back in 1990s British youth slang. It's also worth noting that, by mid-2018, texting was being rivalled in popularity by voice-messaging, touted as faster and "more human" than typing.[22])

The *later* here is not, once again, the later of procrastination, the endless deferral of tasks that typically descends into shame spirals and action-paralysis. It is the later of the looming but mostly ungraspable question: why do anything at all? What can possibly be the ways of going on when boredom seems so often to intimate that there is no reason to go on? "*Hier ist kein warum,*" a Nazi prison guard notoriously said to Primo Levi when the latter asked why the guard had knocked an icicle out of Levi's dry mouth. "Here there is no why." Boredom is not a concentration camp, to be sure, but it can feel profoundly torturous and imprisoning after its own fashion. As in an actual prison, meaning is systematically erased from the world we inhabit, and along with it the very capacity for making meaning. We feel the need to break out; but we precisely won't do it by overpowering boredom with more titillation and distraction. No, other strategies must be executed.

LOVE

We must now, as they say in parliamentary debates, call the question. I have argued that the real stakes in boredom are political, not simply personal. Michael E. Gardiner's notion of semiocapitalism is once more useful for present purposes. "Might boredom, then, in some small way help to protect us from the threat of chaos, the annihilation of meaning that semiocapitalism always teeters on the brink of?" Gardiner wonders. "Could it allow us to at least envisage the possibility of hitching ourselves to the 'slow horse of meaning,' rather than being simply overwhelmed by the hermeneutical nihilism of info-capitalism?"[23] Let us unpack this a bit. What Gardiner calls semiocapitalism is another way of expressing at least part of what I mean by the Interface and neoliberal boredom – that is, the way we interact with the economic and social systems of the current arrangement, especially as delivered to everyday experience by digital-service surrounds such as Alexa or by screens that are so commonly at our fingertips. The term *semiocapitalism* is preferable to the (apparently equivalent?) locution used in the next sentence of Gardiner's essay, *info-capitalism,* because the issue is not really information but meaning itself. Capitalism's repeated implication of our desires is a matter of how we are placed in systems of signs, not data. Data are abstractions; signs offer immersive and inescapable experience – even as the meaning we desire, emancipatory meaning, is drained from the body politic like blood from a bullet-riddled corpse.

It is the relentless circulation of signs without definitive meaning that opens up the annihilation to which Gardiner refers. Thus, for example, we are surrounded not just by social media feeds and feedback loops, but also by "memes" and constant imagistic meta-combinations that, once upon a Situationist time, might have been considered liberating but now are no more than cute distractions. There is a potential and rather depressing analysis of what "cute" might mean in such a context, especially since the experience of cute objects and images is itself a kind of brain-drug, a dopamine rush facilitated by YouTube videos and posted GIFs of frolicking or funny animals. Cuteness-craving "is kind of a vice," one social psychologist has noted, comparing the desire to sugar or sex in its instinctual power over more rational or self-controlled states of mind. "We want our cute fix … It's something that gives us pleasure and makes us come back."[24]

Drugs are the perpetual enemies of reason, enablers of the vice of incontinence – so much has been obvious since the first discussions of *akrasia* (ἀκρασία), or weakness of the will, among the ancient Greek philosophers. We have likewise come to appreciate that drugs come in many forms, not just mind- or mood-altering chemicals. Can philosophical analysis of boredom really help us here? Gardiner has in a way just updated the familiar philosophical position that boredom is instructive of one's existential position. It might, if we cease to flee its dark embrace, slow us down enough to appreciate the dangers of real nihilism that lie on the far side of addictive stimulation. New language, but old point. Sure, let us slow things down so that we can confront the desire-paradoxes that configure boredom and its attendants. But does that change anything about the system?

I take leave to doubt it, though doing so gives me little pleasure, critical or otherwise. "Admittedly," Gardiner admits, "boredom understood in this way might be a necessary but not sufficient condition for the realisation of genuinely transformative social possibilities." Moreover, "we must accept that purely individual adaptations, self-help techniques and sincere (if largely ineffectual) resistances are destined to fail, because they do not go beyond the confines of our privatised and commodified life experiences." Exactly! "Put differently, there can only be collective solutions to the libidinal disinvestments that boredom might represent."[25] Again, exactly!

But once more we must unpack the rather heavy luggage of jargon and theory in play here. In other words, boredom pumps the brakes on the runaway obliterations of meaning so typical of the swipe-left regime, even as it reveals that the problem is not you, the user. The problem is, rather, the Interface, which is a structural and economic reality that must submit to further philosophical analysis. But does that analysis counter the nihilism we sense here? Rather not, unfortunately; or at least not by itself. I think, instead, that we must embrace, like Nietzsche, the reality of nihilism: that the only meaning in the world is of our creation. And now we must ask the hardest question of all: is there a collective solution of the kind that Gardiner (and others) has demanded for the new versions of boredom we encounter in the twenty-first century?

Like so many others, I am forever haunted by Schopenhauer's vision of boredom as calling forth the "countenance of real despair." The boredom of soldiers, prisoners, homeless people, and other abject persons does indeed make a mockery of the teenaged or over-entitled subject who is obsessed with a touch-screen. And yet, we cannot simply dismiss the commonalities to be discerned here. The tragedy of human existence is called forth in circumstances both miserable and comfortable.[26] That is the way of things. Long ago – as it now seems to me, though it was just a flicker in cosmic terms – I argued, in common with many other philosophers, that happiness was the wrong pursuit for human beings.[27] Or, to be more precise, I argued that "How can I be happy?" is the right question but it is mostly pursued wrongly, without taking adequate account of social and political context. Happiness is a structural phenomenon, not an individual one. Thus there is something essentially fearful and fugitive about the ceaseless attempt to evade an absence of stimulation by filling it with whatever stimulus is ready to hand. The project self-defeats. This is the happiness equivalent of empty calories: we all know junk food is delicious but lacking in nutritional value. We eat it anyway because it offers short-term fulfillment of ever-present cravings hard-wired into our frames, for fat, sugar, and salt. Empty calories are still calories, of course, and double the damage they inflict on us by creating cycles of desire. I acquire a *taste* for potato chips or soft drinks, almost a dependency. Happiness conceived on a desire-fulfillment model is like binge-eating french fries or binge-watching Netflix. It might feel good in the moment, but there is likely to be regret later.

I think this critique of pervasive confusion about happiness is still valid. I likewise think that some conceptual clarity about the nature of happiness can aid us in altering life patterns to appreciate the social and political challenges at hand. My original conclusion was broadly Aristotelian: happiness as desire-fulfillment must be replaced with notions of virtue and contemplation, the right actions arising from a contented inner spirit. Nothing in the meantime has changed that view; indeed, as the mechanisms of desire-arousal and (alleged) desire-fulfillment have become more sophisticated, and our immersion in technology more thorough, so our need to think through the pathologies of everyday life has become more urgent. Happiness of some kind remains within our grasp, but not because we can overmaster our desires, the restlessness of wanting that makes boredom such a bugbear of the Interface. Rather, because as Freud noticed, and as Debord and others recall to us, our desires can be bent and curved into novel, liberating shapes. We can drift and wander, not lost, not bored, but open to the experience of life. We empty our minds of stress and striving, and find a peace within ourselves where there are no specific goals, no unrealized plans, no paradoxical tangles of futile wishing for a desire.

No goals, but still a purpose. The cessation of desire is death; life is, by contrast, desire that is not in conflict with itself. Perceive that, and you will never be bored again. Or … or … if you are bored, you will know, as all the greatest philosophers of the condition have, that this is an opportunity, a moment of insight. The rest is up to you. Don't swipe. No: dwell, wonder, reflect, and above all enjoy your symptom – for you have nothing else to enjoy. As Debord advised, we are all learning *how to wait*. It is our condition, our context, and our crisis all at once. Boredom gives the sign, but only we can provide the solution. Why would you need to wish any other desire again?

Are there collective solutions here? I honestly cannot say, though I will suggest that the project of constant criticism – of oneself and the structures that scaffold selfhood – is the best we can do. This is what I understand as philosophy.

The project of endless seeking after happiness is revealed, in the very same instant as we feel its imperious energy, as one of relentless unhappiness. We cannot escape ourselves, and our consciousness, any more than we can escape our desires. Manage them, perhaps. Maybe constrain or shape them, as we might do likewise to the physical aspects of our existence. But no better than that. Accepting these truths is what it is, I think, to love oneself.

DEATH

For, as we all know but desperately try to forget, mortality is the real condition of which boredom can never be regarded as more than a symptom.

And so we come to the end. I could go on, but I would not want to bore you. No one here gets out alive, and yet we must all learn how to wait. There is no swiping those truths off your screen. Neoliberal boredom, which flees the self forever in those desperate bouts of consumption that have become so familiar, must be transformed into the philosophical boredom where the feelings of stall and stasis, the routine irritations of having nothing to do, instead open up vistas of reflection. Even here, the vicious circle still encloses us. Self-reflection is a dangerous pursuit: the gift of consciousness is, after all, also a burden. There is no cure for that.

A book, by its nature, offers the reader a linear experience – a form, we might say, of voluntary enchainment. To be sure, we can read selectively or in bursts, but the sentence as a mechanism always pushes us forward. But as Žižek has said of narrative itself, "The experience of a linear 'organic' flow of events" is a species of necessary illusion.[28] Thoughts, like events and actions, can be *disciplined* into a straight line by setting them down in lines, but thoughts are unruly: they will always contrive to evade the strictures of reliable forward progress. Žižek suggests that the only way to reveal the unconscious acceptance of the illusions of forwardness is to "proceed in a reverse way," by chopping and counter-channelling the narrative in the manner of Harold Pinter's *Betrayal* (play 1978; film version 1983) or the haunting Christopher Nolan film *Memento* (2000). Sometimes the end really is the beginning. Certainly when a book's final argument winds back to its initial prompt, it may be that the apparent forward progress has been in fact a succession of circles rather than a straight line.

We should recall that an argument that runs in a circle is not necessarily a circular argument; and anyway, a circular argument is technically a valid one (the conclusion invariably follows from the premises). To make the argument sound, we must also demonstrate that the premises are true. At least some of the present ones are demonstrably so. Boredom is experienced as an affliction. We most often seek to flee or destroy it. Our efforts are doomed to fail. Worse, they entangle us in economies of desire and attention that may prove actively harmful to selfhood and happiness.

Even when we have done our necessary social and cultural due diligence, however, exposing the mechanisms that prey upon our own weakness of will, the primordial experience of boredom remains. It cannot be explained away, it must be confronted. And that confrontation entails a mortal struggle. According to Socrates and the Stoics, death returns us to a condition of non-being no different from the time before life. Even if we fancy some sort of existence after death – I do not – this life as we currently know will undoubtedly cease at some future point. And this truth is as inescapable to human consciousness as is the very existence of that consciousness.

The French "anti-humanist" philosopher Louis Althusser, a notorious depressive and intellectual fraud, confessed to the murder of his wife, Hélène Rytmann, on the very first page of his extraordinary posthumous autobiography, *L'avenir dure longtemps* (the book was published in 1992; Althusser died in 1990). It is a shocking story, of what began as an uxorious neck massage and ended in a half-intended strangulation. "Hélène's features are serene and motionless, her open eyes gazing up at the ceiling. And suddenly I'm terror-stricken: her eyes have glazed over as if forever and a tiny portion of her tongue is visible, strange and calm, between her lips and her teeth. I've seen dead people before, to be sure, but never in my life have I seen the face of a strangled woman. I nevertheless know she's been strangled. But how? I stand up and I cry out, 'I've strangled Hélène.'"[29] Indeed you have, sir.

Althusser never went to trial for the murder and was, instead, sent to a psychiatric clinic where he ended his days. His book, the longest of a long career, confesses misdeeds high and low, including his endemic fraudulence in pretending knowledge of classical texts he had never read. (He says he "knew a little Spinoza, nothing about Aristotle, the Sophists and the Stoics, quite a lot about Plato and Pascal, nothing about Kant, a bit about Hegel, and finally a few passages of Marx.") Critics have suggested that the sheer self-destructiveness of the text presented a case of "posthumous suicide."[30] The title, which hints at the depression and boredom from which the philosopher suffered through most of life, has been variously translated as "The Future Lasts a Long Time" (literal but clunky) and "The Future Lasts Forever" (better, though *longtemps* is rendered with poetic licence). Either way, one feels the heavy weight of time here. *L'avenir*, meanwhile, is indeed the future, but so is *la future* – a nuance unavailable in English, except that most handy online translator-bots will render the former as "the future" and the latter as "The Future." This titular endorsement captures the connotation of *la future* as a looming objective presence, a wall of time, while *l'avenir* is what is to come.

Why dwell on such a macabre series of incidents? Althusser is the extreme case of what visits almost all of us: the severe self-doubt of who we are. Not many would follow in conceiving a philosophy of anti-humanism, which suggests that human agency is an illusion given the vast network of "ideological state apparatuses" that entangle and dominate us, let alone indulging in systematic professional deception and spouse-murder. But most of us have wondered, at moments, why we are here at all and what we can do about it. These are, after all, considered basic philosophical questions. How can we stop being ghosts to ourselves, revenants of our own ceaseless, infinitely repeated longing? As our time together comes to an end, because even circular books made straight do not last forever, we must ask: What is to come, and how should we go on? At this juncture, *l'avenir* meets *savoir attendre*. Time hangs heavy on our hands, again and always; and yet life is all too brief. Both are true.

Boredom is the sign that we are ever in the presence of death; but it is also, in the same moment, an urgent endorsement of life. Desire is tangled, stalled, self-contradictory, violent, or mired in addiction.

This is not the end of the world but its beginning. We can truly find ourselves again in boredom. We can discover what we temporarily lost, that is, knowing what to do with ourselves. This is the way to go on, my friends. It is time to live! It is, again and always, that time and no other.

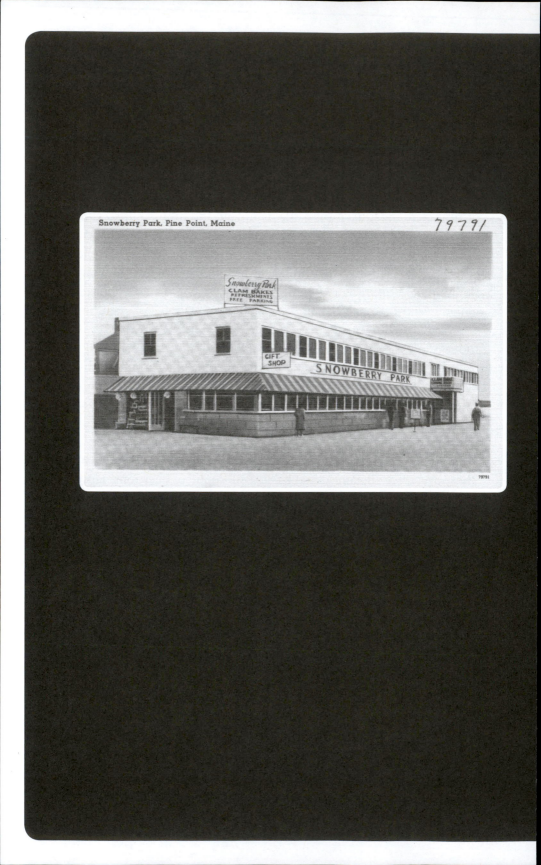

Snowberry Park, Pine Point, Maine

79791

ACKNOWLEDGMENTS

The critical act in its essence constitutes
the refusal of boredom.

Patricia Meyer Spacks, *Boredom* (1996)

Writing this short book has proven a lively and challenging under-taking. My sincere thanks go first and foremost to Khadija Coxon, of McGill-Queen's University Press, who has been a collaborator and champion of this book from its beginning. Her suggestions for revisions large and small shape every part of the text, and indeed the main lines of argument have been developed through our con-versations. This book is inconceivable without her efforts.

Parts of the book draw from material that has been published in early and somewhat different form: "Boredom and the Origin of Philosophy" in *The Boredom Studies Reader: Frameworks and Perspectives*, ed. Michael E. Gardiner and Julian Jason Haladyn (London: Routledge, 2016); *Social Media and Your Brain*, ed. Carlos Prado (Santa Barbara, CA: Praeger, 2016); and "Truth, Interpretation, and Addiction to Conviction," in *America's Post-Truth Phenomenon: When Feelings and Opinions Trump Facts and Evidence*, ed. Carlos Prado (Santa Barbara, CA: Praeger, 2018). I thank the editors for their invitations to address the urgent topics of boredom, addiction, and technology. Some small parts of the text were first published in the *Literary Review of Canada* and the *Globe and Mail*. My thanks to Sarmishta Subramanian and Natasha Hassan, respectively.

Discussion with many friends and colleagues has informed my thinking on the issues addressed here. Thanks especially to Molly Sauter, Josh Glenn, Simon Gelndinning, Arthur Kroker, Juan Pablo Bermudèz-Rey, and Carlos Prado. Two anonymous readers for the press offered a number of helpful suggestions. Elspeth Gibson assisted with bibliographic research; Wendy Calderone and Mary Newberry executed the endgame.

There is no evidence that Freud, elsewhere on record as a confirmed dog person, ever uttered the much-repeated line "Time spent with cats is never wasted." Why, he might ask, do we *wish* that he had said it? Would that make cats stand higher in the world of meaning? We can only speculate. I will paraphrase and say that time spent with *my* cats is never boring; their sly presence informs this work. Finally I am grateful to Molly Montgomery, always and forever, for her boundless support and love.

NOTES

Preface

1 Martin Parr, *Boring Postcards*, rev. ed. (London: Phaidon, 2004).

2 See Luc Sante, *Folk Photography: The American Real-Photo Postcard, 1905–1930* (Portland, OR: Yeti Publishing, 2010).

3 This is why the idea of living in an airport is essentially bizarre, if not also comic. The 2004 Steven Spielberg comedy-drama *The Terminal*, starring Tom Hanks, depicts the life of man stuck at New York's John F. Kennedy Airport after he is denied entry into the United States. He cannot return home because of a civil war and quickly adapts to a furtive life in the non-place of the airport. The story is based in part on the real case of Mehran Karimi Nasseri, an Iranian refugee who lived in Terminal One of Paris's Charles de Gaulle Airport for eighteen years, from 1988 to 2006. In 2018, of course, there is no shred of comedy left in considering the fate of refugees turned back from the US border but not able to return to war-torn home countries. Instead of airport terminals, we have concentration camps at the US-Mexico border.

4 Slavoj Žižek dwells at some length on the architecture of the motel in *Psycho* in a section of his *Enjoy Your Symptom! Jacques Lacan in Hollywood and Out* (New York: Routledge, 2013). He writes, "If the Bates Motel were to be built by [Frank] Gehry, directly combining the old mother's house and the flat modern motel into a new hybrid entity, there would have been no need for Norman to kill his victims, since he would have been relieved of the unbearable

tension that compels him to run between the two places – he would have a third place of mediation between the two extremes" (273). The point is repeated in *The Pervert's Guide to Cinema* (dir. Sophie Fiennes, 2006). I discuss this notion of tension between vertical and horizontal, riffing on the Žižek fancy of a Gehry-designed hybrid, in Kingwell, "Frank's Motel: Horizontal and Vertical in the Big Other," in *The Ends of History: Questioning the Stakes of Historical Reason*, ed. Joshua Nichols and Amy Swiffen, 103–26 (New York: Routledge, 2013); also published as a stand-alone illustrated pamphlet (San Francisco: Blurb, 2013).

5 Victor Pineiro, "Navigating the 'Hotel California' Effect of Social Platforms," *Digiday* (17 April 2015), https://digiday.com/marketing/navigating-hotel-california-effect-social-platforms/. "Social platforms are now built to breed separation anxiety: every new feature designed to keep you on the platform longer, taking in its content (and its ads)," Pineiro writes. "We don't want to leave these platforms. We want to be stuck in the Hotel California, prisoners of our own device." The play on "device" and "devices" is inevitable here, and so maybe even forgivable.

6 György Lukács, preface to *The Theory of the Novel: A Historico-Philosophical Essay on the Forms of Great Epic Literature*, trans. Anna Bostock (London: Merlin, 1962). Stuart Jeffries takes the phrase as the title for his comprehensive account of the Frankfurt school. See Jeffries, *Grand Hotel Abyss: The Lives of the Frankfurt School* (London: Verso, 2016).

7 Martin Heidegger, *Being and Time*, trans. John Macquarrie and Edward Robinson (London: Blackwell, 1962), 173.

Part One

1 In addition to general works already cited in the annotated bibliography, one might mention here the following: Elizabeth Goodstein, *Experience without Qualities: Boredom and Modernity* (Stanford, CA: Stanford University Press, 2005); Barbara Dalle Pezze and Carlo Salzani, eds, *Essays on Boredom and Modernity*

(New York: Rodolphi, 2008); and Michael E. Gardiner and Julian Jason Haladyn, eds, *The Boredom Studies Reader: Frameworks and Perspectives* (London: Routledge, 2016). I would also single out Patricia Meyer Spacks's detailed study of boredom in English literature from the eighteenth century to today, *Boredom: The Literary History of a State of Mind* (Chicago: University of Chicago Press, 1996). Spacks is especially illuminating on how women, especially in domestic scenes found in early English novels, experience boredom and its possible reactions quite differently than do men, in particular not always having action available to them as the morally imperative response to *accidie* or ennui.

2 Chris Cillizza, "How the Senate's Tech Illiteracy Saved Mark Zuckerbeg," CNN.com (11 April 2018), https://www.cnn.com/2018/04/10/politics/mark-zuckerberg-senate-hearing-tech-illiteracy-analysis/index.html.

3 See *Theaetetus* 155c–d, and *Meno*, 84c. It is disputed whether the wonder referred to in these dialogues is mere intellectual perplexity, the kind that arouses philosophical interest, or a more robust notion of wonder in the sense of awe. We know, however, that the traditional view of wonder as the prompt to philosophical and scientific reflection has a long pedigree since Plato, including such figures as Bacon and Husserl. My own account of this aspect of reflection is outlined in Kingwell, "Husserl's Sense of Wonder," *Philosophical Forum* 31, no. 1 (Spring): 85–107; reprinted in Kingwell, *Practical Judgments* (Toronto: University of Toronto Press, 2002), 63–94.

4 Ludwig Wittgenstein, *Tractatus Logico-Philosophicus*, trans. David Pears and Brian McGuinness (London: Routledge, 1961), prop. 6.4311.

5 Adam Phillips, "On Being Bored," in *On Kissing, Tickling, and Being Bored: Psychoanalytic Essays on the Unexamined Life* (Cambridge, MA: Harvard University Press, 1993), 68.

6 Erich Fromm, *Man for Himself: An Inquiry into the Psychology of Ethics* (New York: Routledge, 1999), 40.

7 Erich Fromm, *The Dogma of Christ* (New York: Holt, Rinehart & Winston, 1955), 181.

8 Arthur Schopenhauer, *The World as Will and Representation* (*Die Welt als Wille und Vorstellung*, 1811, 1844), 1:313.

9 For more on this, see Lars Svendsen, *A Philosophy of Boredom* (New York: Reaktion Books, 2005); and for some further analysis of how boredom relates to work and leisure, Joshua Glenn and Mark Kingwell, *The Idler's Glossary* (Windsor: Biblioasis, 2008); and Glenn and Kingwell, *The Wage Slave's Glossary* (Windsor: Biblioasis, 2011).

One can compare Kierkegaard on the general point: "Whatever can be the meaning of this life? If we divide mankind into two large classes, we can say that one works for a living, the other has no need to. But working for one's living can't be the meaning of life; to suppose that constantly procuring the conditions of life should be the answer to the question of the meaning of what they make possible is a contradiction. Usually the lives of the other class have no meaning either, beyond that of consuming the said conditions. To say that the meaning of life is to die seems again to be a contradiction." Søren Kierkegaard, *Either/Or: A Fragment of Life*, trans. Alastair Hannay (Harmondsworth: Penguin Books, 2004), 49. Later, he will add this gloss: "Idleness as such is by no means a root of evil; quite the contrary, it is a truly divine way of life so long as one is not bored" (230).

10 Kierkegaard, *Either/Or*, 227.

11 Ibid., 228.

12 Søren Kierkegaard, *The Concept of Irony: With Continual Reference to Socrates*, trans. Howard V. Hong and Edna H. Hong (Princeton: Princeton University Press, 1961), 302.

13 A good discussion of the point can be found in Gregor Malantschuk, *Kierkegaard's Thought*, trans. Howard V. Hong and Edna H. Hong (Princeton: Princeton University Press, 1971), 205.

14 Arthur Schopenhauer, *Parerga and Paralipomena* (1851), 2:293.

15 Martin Heidegger, *The Fundamental Concepts of Metaphysics: World, Finitude, Solitude*, trans. William McNeill and Nicholas Walker (Bloomington, IN: Indiana University Press, 1995); all subsequent citations are to this edition.

16 Ibid., 78.

17 Ibid., 80.

18 Ibid., 80.

19 Kingsley Amis, *Difficulties with Girls* (London: Summit, 1998), 197.

20 Edward St Aubyn, *The Complete Patrick Melrose Novels* (London: Picador, 2012), 91.

21 Ibid., 112.

22 Martin Amis, *Night Train* (New York: Vintage, 2007), 120.

23 Ibid., 173.

24 As Homer Simpson memorably described it.

25 Heidegger, *Fundamental Concepts*, 105.

26 Ibid., 109.

27 Ibid., 132.

28 Ibid., 137.

29 Ibid., 140.

30 Ibid., 152.

31 Ibid., 153.

32 Ibid., 154.

33 Ibid., 161.

34 Theodor W. Adorno, "Free Time," in *The Culture Industry: Selected Essays on Mass Culture*, ed. and trans. R.M. Bernstein (New York: Routledge, 1991); all further citations are from this edition.

35 Ibid., 191.

36 Ibid., 192.

37 Ibid., 187.

38 Ibid., 194.

39 Ibid., 188.

40 Ibid., 189.

41 Pierre Bourdieu, *Distinction: A Social Critique of the Judgment of Taste*, trans. Richard Nice (Cambridge, MA: Harvard University Press, 1984).

42 Matthew de Abaitua, *The Art of Camping* (London: Hamish Hamilton, 2011).

43 Adorno, "Free Time," 191.

44 Ibid., 191.

45 Ibid., 192.

46 Ibid., 192.

47 See Sandi Mann and Rebekah Cadman, "Does Being Bored Make

Us More Creative?" *Creative Research Journal* 26, no. 2 (2014): 166. This article cites and summarizes most of the recent psychological literature on the topic. Its central conclusion: The evidence "suggests that boredom can sometimes be a force for good. This means that it might be a worthwhile enterprise to allow or even embrace boredom in work, education, and leisure. On an individual basis, if one is trying to solve a problem or come up with creative solutions, the findings from our studies suggest that undertaking a boring task (especially a reading task) might help with coming up with a more creative outcome" (171).

48 Ibid., 171.

49 Timothy Williamson, *The Philosophy of Philosophy* (New York: Wiley-Blackwell, 2008), 288. All subsequent quotations are from the same passage.

50 P.M.S. Hacker, "A Philosopher of Philosophy: Critical Notice of *The Philosophy of Philosophy*," *Philosophical Inquiry* 59 (April 2009): 337–48. Hacker's savage review, not at all boring, concludes with this fearsome paragraph:

> *The Philosophy of Philosophy* fails to characterize the linguistic turn in analytic philosophy. It fails to explain why many of the greatest analytic philosophers thought philosophy to be a conceptual investigation. It does not explain what a conceptual truth is or was taken to be, but mistakenly assimilates conceptual truths to analytic ones. It holds that philosophy can discover truths about reality by reflection alone, but does not explain how. It holds that some philosophical truths are confirmable by experiments, but does not say which. It misrepresents the methodology of the empirical sciences and the differences between the sciences and philosophy. It has nothing whatsoever to say about most branches of philosophy. But it does provide an adequate "self-image" of the way Professor Williamson does philosophy.

51 English translation is from Guy Debord, *Society of the Spectacle* (Detroit: Black & Red, 1983), sec. 220.

52 Friedrich Nietzsche, *Twilight of the Idols*, with *Ecce Homo* and *The Antichrist*, trans. Antony M. Ludovici (New York: Wordsworth Classics, 2007), 141.

53 T.S. Eliot, "Burnt Norton," in *Four Quartets* (London: Faber and Faber, 1944), 99–103. Compare Marina van Zuylen, *The Plenitude of Distraction* (New York: Sequence, 2017). Van Zuylen's book is a celebration of unplanned thought and wandering ideas, and its heroes are the creatively distracted: Montaigne, Nietzsche, Proust, Bergson, and others. As a great believer in strolling both physical and mental, as well as a dedicated purveyor of the unexpected aside and loose connection, I must commend this wayward course of thought. On the other hand, it is hardly productive to be (say) shopping for clothes, checking your phone, and playing Tetris even while you are supposed to be listening to a lecture. True distraction is a discipline; the rest is just a non-clinical form of attention deficit disorder.

54 Phillips, "On Being Bored."

55 Peter Toohey, *Boredom: A Lively History* (New Haven, CT: Yale University Press, 2012).

56 Jennifer Egan, "Pure Language," in *A Visit from the Goon Squad* (New York: Anchor, 2010). Rebecca, wife of the aging protagonist of this near-future (year 2021) section of Egan's novel, is the source of the notion. Rebecca, the narrator tells us, "was an academic star. Her new book was on the phenomenon of word-casings, a term she'd invented for words that no longer had meaning outside quotation marks. English was full of these empty words – 'friend' and 'real' and 'story' and 'change' – words that had been shucked of their meanings and reduced to husks. Some, like 'identity,' 'search,' and 'cloud,' had clearly been drained of life by their Web usage. With others, the reasons were more complex; how had 'American' become an ironic term? How had 'democracy' come to be used in such an arch, mocking way?" (323–4).

57 See, for example, Slavoj Žižek, *Looking Awry: An Introduction to Jacques Lacan through Popular Culture* (Cambridge, MA: MIT Press, 1991).

58 Mark Kingwell, *Unruly Voices* (Windsor: Biblioasis, 2012), 16.

59 Jia Tolentino, "The Gig Economy Celebrates Working Yourself to Death," *New Yorker*, 22 March 2017, https://www.newyorker.com/culture/jia-tolentino/

the-gig-economy-celebrates-working-yourself-to-death.
Most commentary on the gig economy has been positive: an
"entrepreneurial dream," one books yodels, while others offer tips on
creative ways to get better and more lucrative gigs.

60 David Graeber, *Bullshit Jobs: A Theory* (New York: Simon & Schuster,
2018); Graeber originally addressed the issue and popularized the
term – long used by workers themselves, of course – in "On the
Phenomenon of Bullshit Jobs: *A Work Rant*," *Strike! Magazine*
(August 2013), https://strikemag.org/bullshit-jobs/.

61 Drew Hendricks, "12 Tips for Being Happy at a Boring Job," *Inc.* (26
January 2015), https://www.inc.com/drew-hendricks/12-tips-you-
can-be-happy-at-a-boring-job.html. One is forced to point out that
in this cheery article *leaving the boring job* is not countenanced as a
possibility. I guess that might be Tip #13?

62 Rosecrans Baldwin, "Throw Away Your Earbuds, Boredom Is
Good," *Los Angeles Times*, 7 February 2016, http://www.latimes.com/
opinion/op-ed/la-oe-0207-baldwin-boredom-benefits-20160207-
story.html.

63 *Citizens United v Federal Election Commission*, 558 US 310 (2010).
I offer some analysis of the political implications of the decision in
the introduction to *Unruly Voices* and return to the case later in the
present book as well.

64 Thorsten Veblen, *The Theory of the Leisure Class: An Economic Study
in the Evolution of Institutions* (1899); Edith Wharton, *The House
of Mirth* (1905); Wharton, *The Custom of the Country* (1913); and
Wharton, *The Age of Innocence* (1920). (In this and the next citation,
I have not given edition information for widely accessible texts.)

65 Max Horkheimer and Theodor Adorno, "The Culture Industry:
Enlightenment as Mass Deception," in *Dialectic of Enlightenment*,
trans. John Cumming (New York: Herder and Herder, 1972); F. Scott
Fitzgerald, *The Beautiful and Damned* (1922); Fitzgerald, *The Great
Gatsby* (1925); but especially Fitzgerald, *Tender Is the Night* (1934).

66 For example, Slavoj Žižek, *For They Know Not What They Do:
Enjoyment as a Political Factor* (London: Verso, 2008); David Foster
Wallace, *Infinite Jest* (Boston: Little, Brown/Back Bay Books, 1996).

67 On the first point see, for example, Mark Fisher, *Capitalist Realism: Is*

There No Alternative? (London [?]: Zero Books, 2009), which argues
that, far from initiating widespread crisis, the financial meltdown of
2008 only further entrenched capitalist interests and ideology.

68 See, for example, "What Toronto Singles Love (and Hate) about
Dating in the City," *Toronto Star*, 9 February 2016, http://www.
thestar.com/life/relationships/2016/02/09/what-singles-love-and-
hate-about-dating-in-toronto.html.

The "commodification" and "hollowing-out" of tech-based dating
apps was mentioned by several people interviewed for this article.
One single person quoted there predicted that "2016 should be
the year of dating off the grid." But there are micro-generational
differences to be noted here, with the singles quoted in the article
above mainly lying within a demographic of twenty-five and more.
They also live in a large city where other dating opportunities were
possible (many of them mentioned preferring to meet new people
in bars or through networks of friends). One early 2016 article
on National Public Radio's online magazine noted that the use of
dating apps by American eighteen- to twenty-four-year-olds had
tripled since 2013, according to a Pew Research Center study. See
Jennifer Ludden, "Do You Like Me? Swiping Leads to Spike in
Online Dating for Young Adults," The Two-Way, 11 February 2016,
http://www.npr.org/sections/thetwo-way/2016/02/11/466342716/
do-you-like-me-swiping-leads-to-spike-in-online-dating-for-young-
adults?utm_source=nextdraft&utm_medium=email.

One special problem for Torontonians, at least according to one
critic, might be that they live in "the most fascinatingly boring city in
the world." But this turns out to be a good thing. "History in Toronto
does not bend toward justice. It bends towards the hot tub," Stephen
Marche wrote in the *Guardian*, 4 July 2016. "There is something
radical about these people leading their quiet lives out together,
without much fuss." The key question for the city "is whether the
city will rise into a glorious future of a mingled and complicated
humanity, an avatar of a singular cosmopolitanism, or whether it
will shrink back and be swallowed by the provincial miasma that
inveigles it." https://www.theguardian.com/cities/2016/jul/04/
new-toronto-most-fascinatingly-boring-city-guardian-canada-week.

69 Eddington's book *The Nature of the Physical World*, based on his 1926–27 Gifford Lectures, was published in 1935 (London: Macmillan). In it he defends his controversial "idealist" view that "the stuff of the world is mind stuff." Benjamin quotes Eddington at length, saying "one can virtually Kafka speak" in his prose; see "Some Reflections on Kafka," in *Illuminations*, ed. Hannah Arendt, trans. Harry Zohn (New York: Schocken), 141–2.

70 Doree Shafir, "Meet the People Who Listen to Podcasts Crazy-Fast," Buzzfeed, 12 November 2017, https://www.buzzfeed.com/doree/ meet-the-people-who-listen-to-podcasts-at-super-fast-speeds?utm_ term=.majrNrz1N#.lj6lwlAXw.

71 Neil Levy, "Autonomy and Addiction," *Canadian Journal of Philosophy* 36, no. 3 (September 2006): 432, 431.

72 Ibid., 433.

73 Dan Kavanagh, *Going to the Dogs* (London: Viking, 1987), 76. The book is one in a series of comic detective stories featuring a bisexual former policeman called Duffy; Kavanagh is the pen name of novelist Julian Barnes.

74 Irvine Welsh, *Trainspotting* (London: Secker & Warburg, 1993); the film adaptation was directed by Danny Boyle (1996).

Part Two

1 David Remnick, "The Unwinding of Donald Trump," *New Yorker*, 17 July 2018, https://www.newyorker.com/news/daily-comment/ the-unwinding-of-donald-trump.

2 Sam Dolnick, "The Man Who Knew Too Little," *New York Times*, 10 March 2018, https://www.nytimes.com/2018/03/10/style/the-man- who-knew-too-little.html?smid=fb-nytimes&smtyp=cur.

3 See Farhad Manjoo, "We Have Reached Peak Screen, Now Revolution Is in the Air," *New York Times*, 27 June 2018, https://www. nytimes.com/2018/06/27/technology/peak-screen-revolution.html.

4 William Wan, "I Had a Bit of an App Addiction. Until These Apps Saved Me," *Washington Post*, 29 June 2018, https://www.washingtonpost.com/news/to-your-health/

wp/2018/06/29/i-had-a-bit-of-an-app-addiction-until-these-apps-saved-me/?utm_term=.a7f39b0a181f.

5 Jaron Lanier, *Ten Arguments for Deleting Your Social Media Accounts Now* (New York: Henry Holt, 2018).

6 Alice G. Walton, "Social Media May Be More Harmful to Girls Than Boys, Study Finds," *Forbes Magazine*, 20 March 2018, https://www.forbes.com/sites/alicegwalton/2018/03/20/social-media-may-be-more-psychologically-harmful-to-girls-than-boys/#79b998f97e35.

7 Consider the book *I Feel Better after I Type to You* (Superbunker, 2006), an unedited 254-page collection of AOL search queries entered by user 23187425 from May 2006. The poetic, even elegiac quality of this found document demonstrates considerable sadness. The search for meaning is collapsed to the mere act of search, the internet itself rendered into a kind of spectral second-person addressee ("You") even as the user is known publicly only as a user number. My thanks to Khadija Coxon for pointing out this poignant instance of the Interface hard at work.

8 Michael E. Gardiner, "The Multitude Strikes Back? Boredom in an Age of Semiocapitalism," *New Formations* 82 (2014): 29.

9 The latest witless proponent of this false charge is former *New York Times* book critic Michiko Kakutani, whose book *The Death of Truth: Notes on Falsehood in the Age of Trump* (New York: Tim Duggan Books, 2018) is a slipshod attempt to lay the existence of Donald Trump at the feet of postmodern and deconstructionist literary theorists (quite different philosophical projects, by the way, though often confused by the superficial). Postmodernism, she claims, is an artistic movement "I've been reading and writing about for four decades." If so, she was asleep at the switch for much of the time, because her characterization of postmodernism is a gross caricature that bears little relation to the nuanced "incredulity towards meta-narratives" championed by Jean-François Lyotard in *The Postmodern Condition: A Report on Knowledge*, trans. Geoff Bennington and Brian Massumi (Minneapolis: University of Minnesota Press, 1984). One is forced, on this feeble showing, to agree with Jonathan Franzen's dyspeptic 2008 judgment that Kakutani is "the stupidest person in New York City."

10 As quoted by Ron Suskind, "Faith, Certainty and the Presidency of George W. Bush," *New York Times Magazine*, 17 October 2004, https://www.nytimes.com/2004/10/17/magazine/faith-certainty-and-the-presidency-of-george-w-bush.html.

11 *Robert Anderson, "The Rashomon Effect and Communication," Canadian Journal of Communication 41, no. 2 (2016): 250–65.*

12 The works collected in Adorno, *Culture Industry*, include both originary analysis *circa* Adorno's landmark collaboration with Horkheimer, *Dialectic of Enlightenment* (1944), but also later specific – and bilious – forays into television comedy, sunbathing, radio, and the idea of leisure.

13 Roland Barthes, *Mythologies*, trans. Annette Lavers (New York: Farrar, Straus & Giroux, 1972), introduction.

14 Compare Jean Baudrillard, *Simulacra and Simulation*, trans. Sheila Faria Glaser (Ann Arbor: University of Michigan Press, 1994); and Debord, *Society of the Spectacle*.

15 See, e.g., Carl Schmitt, *The Concept of the Political*, rev. ed., trans. George Schwab (Chicago: University of Chicago Press, 2007).

16 Ian Brown, "An Encyclopedia Brown Story: Bound and Determined to Fight for the Facts in the Time of Trump," *Globe and Mail*, 7 July 2017, https://www.theglobeandmail.com/arts/books-and-media/an-encyclopedia-ian-brown-story/article35586033/.

17 Alasdair MacIntyre, *After Virtue: A Study in Moral Theory*, 2nd ed. (South Bend: Notre Dame University Press, 1984).

18 This feels like an argument I have made for most of my academic life, but the elision of the two concepts is apparently ineradicable. See Kingwell, *A Civil Tongue: Justice Dialogue and the Politics of Pluralism* (University Park, PA: Pennsylvania State University Press, 1995). I offer a reverse, collective-action-problem critique of incivility in later iterations of the basic argument. See Kingwell, "'Fuck You' and Other Salutations: Incivility as a Collective Action Problem," in *Civility in Politics and Education*, ed. Deborah Mower and Wade Robison, 44–61 (New York: Routledge, 2012).

19 See, for example, Jodi Dean, "Publicity's Secret," *Political Theory* 29, no. 5 (October 2001): 624–50.

20 A recent study by psychologists Hugo Mercier and Dan Sperber

explores the flimsiness of fact-based argument in influencing people's states of mind. See their work *The Enigma of Reason* (Cambridge, MA: Harvard University Press, 2016), which counters a good deal of more pro-reason research. The issue was accessibly addressed by Elizabeth Kolbert in "Why Facts Don't Change Our Minds," *New Yorker*, 27 February 2017, http://www.newyorker.com/magazine/2017/02/27/why-facts-dont-change-our-minds. I have more to say about this issue in the concluding section of this part.

21 The scaffolding proposal was made in an opinion article for the *Globe and Mail*, "Don't Bother Trying to Understand 'the Other Side,'" *Globe and Mail*, 29 August 2017. It draws on arguments made by, among others, my philosophy colleagues Juan Pablo Bermudèz-Rey and Joseph Heath. See especially Heath, *Enlightenment 2.0* (New York: Harper, 2014), which is considerably more optimistic about rationality than I am. I explore some of the relations between addiction and social media in Kingwell, "Boredom, Subjectivity, and the Interface," *Social Media and Your Brain*, ed. Carlos Prado, 3–25 (Santa Barbara, CA: Praeger, 2016); parts of this article are repurposed and revised in the present book. Regulating social media already happens, of course; and suggestions to extend regulation in scaffolded constraints is no different from any other mechanism we might adopt to control our own addictive behaviour.

22 Kingwell, "Mikhail Bakunin," HiLoBrow, 2014, http://hilobrow.com/2014/05/30/mikhail-bakunin/.

23 Among the febrile responses, which divined far more oppressive motives in my views than I can discern myself, was Burt Schoeppe, "University of Toronto Progressive Professor Wants to Limit Free Speech," *Postmillennial*, 30 August 2017, https://thepostmillennial.com/university-toronto-progressive-professor-wants-limit-free-speech/. Sample quotation: "With this article, Kingwell has accomplished a new betrayal, turning aside from reason and opting for the repression of ideas that we used to associate only with the enemies of democracy." As a friend of mine said in response, "Wow! You've been busy." Some further details can be found in notes below.

24 Amy Davidson Sorkin, "The Anatomy of a Trump Twitter Rant: From Scotland Yard to 'Chain Migration,'" *New Yorker*, 15 September

2017, https://www.newyorker.com/news/amy-davidson-sorkin/
the-anatomy-of-a-trump-twitter-rant-from-scotland-yard-to-chain-
migration.

25 See, for example, Stanley Fish, *There's No Such Thing as Free Speech
… And It's a Good Thing, Too* (New York: Oxford University Press,
1994). As Fish argues there, "When someone observes, as someone
surely will, that anti-harassment codes chill speech, one could reply
that since speech only becomes intelligible against the background
of what isn't being said, the background of what has already been
silenced, the only question is the political one of which speech is
going to be chilled, and, all things considered, it seems a good thing
to chill speech like 'nigger,' 'cunt,' 'kike,' and 'faggot.' And if someone
then says, 'But what happened to free-speech principles?' one could
say … free-speech principles don't exist except as a component in a
bad argument in which such principles are invoked to mask motives
that would not withstand close scrutiny."

For a good overview of recent controversies, especially
on university campuses, see Ira Wells, "The Age of Offence,"
Literary Review of Canada (April 2017), http://reviewcanada.ca/
magazine/2017/04/the-age-of-offence/.

26 It is one of life's neater ironies that the psychologist who popularized
the place of empathy in psychological discourse was capital-*B* Boring
– Edwin G. Boring. See Khadija Coxon, "Reality for the People,"
in *America's Post-Truth Phenomenon: When Feelings and Opinions
Trump Facts and Arguments*, ed. Carlos Prado, 117–20 (Santa
Barbara, CA: Praeger, 2018).

27 I explore the slight prospects of mind change in Kingwell, "'It's
Not Just a Good Idea, It's Law': Rationality, Force, and Changing
Minds," in *Legal Violence and the Limits of Law*, ed. Joshua Nichols
and Amy Swiffen, 1–16 (New York: Routledge, 2016). This is in turn
based on an initial foray, Kingwell, "Changing Minds: The Labyrinth
of Decision," *Primer Stories* 4, no. 1 (29 August 2016), http://
primerstories.com/4/changingminds.

The cherished idea of the free-expression "marketplace of ideas,"
meanwhile, is just as subject to failure as any market. In a landmark
1984 article, legal scholar Stanley Ingber called it a "legitimizing

myth." See "The Marketplace of Ideas: A Legitimizing Myth," *Duke Law Journal*, February 1984, 1–91; more recently, commentators have noted how the metaphor values provocation over rational discourse, enabling what Cass Sunstein calls "polarization entrepreneurs" in place of honest traders. A brief survey may be found in Aaron R. Hanlon, "The Myth of the 'Marketplace of Ideas' on Campus," *New Republic*, 6 March 2017, https://newrepublic.com/article/141150/myth-marketplace-ideas-campus-charles-murray-milo-yiannopoulos. Another recent examination of the metaphor's hollowness is David Shih, "Hate Speech and the Misnomer of the 'Marketplace of Ideas,'" NPR, 3 May 2017, http://www.npr.org/sections/codeswitch/2017/05/03/483264173/hate-speech-and-the-misnomer-of-the-marketplace-of-ideas.

28 Kingwell, *Civil Tongue*.

29 See, for example, these two outraged responses to the original published version of the argument. Both focus on one phrase from a 700-word, deliberately polemical article: Ezra Levant, "'We Could Even Ban Media Panel Discussions': Globe & Mail Columnist Calls for Censorship," Rebel, 1 September 2017, https://www.therebel.media/globe_mail_columnist_calls_for_censorship; and Gerry Bowler, "Putting a Muzzle on Those You Disagree With," Troy Media, 1 September 2017, http://troymedia.com/2017/09/01/putting-a-muzzle-on-those-you-disagree-with/.

These media commentators seem particularly exercised by the idea that there might be rational curbs, executed by the people (not the state), on media panel discussions – as if those represent a form of rational debate. "They hate you, my friends," Levant's article concludes. "And they will want to silence you." Hide from the philosopher, friends! He has a muzzle!

An apparently more considered response posted on *Alternative Right* (proudly listed as "The Founding Site of the Alt-Right") laboured to deploy some philosophical reasoning, but just couldn't resist resorting to insults instead of argument: "fraud," "simplistic and nihilistic," "adolescent," "half-clever," and (per contra) "some Harry Potter–reading cat lady writing for slate.com," whatever that means. And so on and on in the usual way, speaking of half-clever. Their screed also included now-familiar deliberate misunderstandings of the original argument, and the presumed sense of grievance at being targeted by "postmodern" and "communist" thought police.

There is also systematic misreading of my positions on morality (I am not an objectivist), ideology (I certainly do not regard it as a settled matter – quite the contrary), and desire (of course it often is irrational – that was my whole point). Anyway, the bottom line is that it's almost as if – and exactly as I argued – these people *actually can't help themselves.* If you are so inclined, see Ryan Andrews, "Free Speech Is Violence, and Its Might Makes Right," *Alternative Right*, 5 September 2017, https://alternativeright.blog/2017/09/05/free-speech-is-violence-and-its-might-makes-right/.

30 See, for example, A.J. Willingham, "The First Amendment Doesn't Guarantee You the Rights You Think It Does," CNN.com, 8 August 2017, http://www.cnn.com/2017/04/27/politics/first-amendment-explainer-trnd/index.html.

31 Call me fanciful, but now I can't help thinking of the 1999 epistemo-action thriller *The Matrix*, starring Keanu Reeves as the illusion-busting saviour-spectre known as Neo. I would even end this section by saying, "Take the red pill," except for the sad fact that the image has been co-opted by angry, Reddit-borne men's rights activists. These geniuses of gender theory think that women *say* they want respect and consideration (blue-pill theory) when what they really want is domination and subjection (red-pill theory). A good critical overview can be found in Rebecca Reid, "Welcome to the Red Pill: The Angry Men's Rights Group That 'Knows What Women Want," *Telegraph*, 13 November 2015, https://www.telegraph.co.uk/women/life/red-pill-mens-rights-anti-feminist-group-who-know-what-women-want/. More recently the mantle of such arguments has been taken on the "incel" (involuntary celibate) movement and the likes of psychologist Jordan Peterson and his followers. OK then, enough said!

32 Elizabeth Kolbert, "Why Facts Don't Change Our Minds," summarizing Mercier and Sperber.

33 Jack Gorman and Sara Gorman, *Denying the Grave: Why We Ignore*

the Facts That Will Save Us (New York: Oxford University Press, 2017), as quoted in Kolbert, "Why Facts Don't Change Our Minds."

34 Steven Sloman and Philip Fernbach, *The Knowledge Illusion: Why We Never Think Alone* (New York: Riverhead, 2017), as quoted in Kolbert, "Why Facts Don't Change Our Minds."

Part Three

1 Matthew Field, "Facebook Will Not Ban Holocaust Denial 'Because People Get Things Wrong,' Says Mark Zuckerberg," *Telegraph*, 18 July 2018, https://www.telegraph.co.uk/technology/2018/07/18/facebook-will-not-ban-holocaust-denial-people-get-things-wrong/.

2 Sheera Frenkel, "Facebook Starts Paying a Price for Scandals," *New York Times*, 25 July 2018, https://www.nytimes.com/2018/07/25/technology/facebook-revenue-scandals.html.

3 Sandy Parakilas, "We Can't Trust Facebook to Regulate Itself," *New York Times*, 19 November 2017, https://www.nytimes.com/2017/11/19/opinion/facebook-regulation-incentive.html. All further Parakilas quotations are from this source.

4 Max Read, "Does Facebook Need a Constitution?," New York Magazine, 18 July 2018, http://nymag.com/selectall/2018/07/does-facebook-need-a-constitution.html.

5 A satirical essay from 2015 had already imagined what "news" would look like once Facebook achieved total control of the feed:

> Before a scheduled interview about his company's new journalism initiative, the wondrous Mark Zuckerberg nobly greeted another dawn yesterday, secure in the knowledge that he is the greatest human being in history and that Facebook is the best thing ever invented. Dashingly handsome, as always, with his Adonis-like physique, Mr Zuckerberg began his day with typical selfless concern for his fellow-man, giving no thought whatsoever to profiting from targeted advertisements for apartment cleaning, discounted for graduates of your college, nor any sort of master plan for global domination achieved by technologically enslaving an anesthetized populace that experiences little beyond compulsive

clicking, swiping, and passively "liking" things. This publication strenuously suggests that misinformed proponents of any such crackpot theories receive capital punishment.
(Teddy Wayne, "Facebook Is the Best," *New Yorker*, 21 May 2015, https://www.newyorker.com/humor/daily-shouts/mark-zuckerberg-is-the-greatest-and-facebook-is-the-best.

6 See Matteo Galizzi and Goerge Lowenstein, "The Soda Tax as a Measure for Sustained Change in Vonsumption," Vox, 14 June 2016, https://voxeu.org/article/beyond-nudging-case-uk-soda-tax.

7 Sarah Kendzior, "Gutting Net Neutrality Is a Death Knell for the Resistance," *Globe and Mail*, 26 November 2017, https://www.theglobeandmail.com/opinion/gutting-net-neutrality-is-a-death-knell-for-the-resistance/article37088279/.

8 It was John Oliver, on HBO's show *Last Week Tonight* – in June 2014, to boot. See Kendzior, "Gutting Net Neutrality." In an earlier part of the segment, Oliver delivered this one-liner: "Net neutrality. The only two words that promised more boredom in the English language are 'featuring Sting.'"

9 John Cassidy, "Why Did the European Commission Fine Google Five Billion Dollars?," *New Yorker*, 20 July 2018, https://www.newyorker.com/news/our-columnists/why-did-the-european-commission-fine-google-five-billion-dollars?

10 Brody Mullins, Rolfe Winkler, and Brent Kendall, "Inside the U.S. Antitrust Probe of Google," *Wall Street Journal*, 19 March 2015, https://www.wsj.com/articles/inside-the-u-s-antitrust-probe-of-google-1426793274.

11 Michael Schulson, "User Behaviour," *Aeon* (Fall 2015), https://aeon.co/essays/if-the-internet-is-addictive-why-don-t-we-regulate-it. See also Natasha Schüll, *Addiction by Design: Machine Gambling in Las Vegas* (Princeton: Princeton University Press, 2012).

12 Natasha Schüll, *Addiction by Design: Machine Gambling in Las Vegas* (Princeton: Princeton University Press, 2012).

13 Laura Noren, "Can Objects Be Evil? A Review of 'Addiction by Design,'" Social Media Collective, 6 September 2012, https://socialmediacollective.org/2012/09/06/addiction-by-design-review/.

14 Maggie Balistreri, *The Evasion-English Dictionary*, rev. ed. (New York: Em Dash Group, 2018).

15 Manjoo, "We Have Reached Peak Screen."

16 Schulson, "User Behavior."

17 Plato's notion of the divided *psyche* runs throughout his work but is especially vivid in *Republic* and *Phaedrus*; the latter dialogue includes, at 246a–54e, the celebrated image of the soul as a chariot with a rational driver attempting to guide two horses, one unruly and one spirited but inclined to nobility. A recent riff on the idea imagines the "individual" mind as the emergent property of a fractious internal committee meeting in which Sleep, Sugar, Water, Protein, and Alcohol (among others) compete for control of the subject's agenda as she moves into Q2 of unemployment. Hallie Cantor, "My Brain: The All-Hands Meeting," *New Yorker*, 24 August 2015, http://www.newyorker.com/magazine/2015/08/24/my-brain-the-all-hands-meeting.

18 Levy, "Autonomy and Addiction," 437 and 442.

19 Ibid., 443.

20 Self-control has lately generated a large academic and popular literature, much of it referencing the celebrated Stanford "marshmallow test," which explores the ability of children to defer gratification and relates that ability to other successful tactics of thought and action, including higher SAT scores and lower Body Mass Index numbers. The most accessible account is Walter Mischel, *The Marshmallow Test: Mastering Self-Control* (Boston: Little, Brown, 2014).

21 See, for example, Tristan Harris, "The Need for a New Design Ethic," a TED Talk archived at http://www.tristanharris.com/the-need-for-a-new-design-ethics/.

22 Joe Edelman, "Choicemaking and the Interface," nxhx.org (July 2014), http://nxhx.org/Choicemaking/.

23 See Rem Koolhaas, *Delirious New York* (New York: Monacelli, 1978); and Jan Gehl, *Cities for People* (Washington, DC: Island, 2010).

24 "I am convinced that boredom is one of the greatest tortures," he wrote in *The Dogma of Christ*. "If I were to imagine Hell, it would be a place where we were constantly bored." Fromm, *The Dogma of*

Christ (New York: Holt, Rinehart & Winston, 1955), 181.

25 Colin Ellard, "Streets with No Game," *Aeon*
(1 September 2015), https://aeon.co/essays/
why-boring-streets-make-pedestrians-stressed-and-unhappy.

26 Rachel Metz, "Your Smartphone Can Tell When
You're Bored," MIT *Technology Review* (2 September
2015), https://www.technologyreview.com/s/540906/
your-smartphone-can-tell-if-youre-bored/.

27 Dean Daley, "The 'Substitute Phone' Is Supposed to Help People with
Smartphone Addiction," *Financial Post*, 28 November 2017, http://
business.financialpost.com/technology/personal-tech/the-substitute-
phone-is-supposed-to-help-people-with-smartphone-addiction.

28 David Foster Wallace, "Laughing with Kafka," *Harper's Magazine*
(July 1998), 23–7.

29 Paul Virilio, *Speed and Politics*, trans. Mark Polizzotti (New York:
Semiotext(e), 2006), 156–7.

30 Annalee Newitz, *Autonomous: A Novel* (New York: Tor, 2018).

31 Ibid., 116.

32 Ibid., 263.

Part Four

1 Jean-Charles Nault, *The Noonday Devil: Acedia, the Unnamed Evil of
Our Times* (San Francisco: Ignatius, 2015), 20, 27.

2 Ibid., 109.

3 Aldous Huxley, "Accidie," in *Mass Leisure*, ed. Eric Larrabee and Rolf
Meyersohn (Glencoe, IL: Free Press, 1956), 18.

4 I address the alleged boredom of baseball in *Fail Better: Why
Baseball Matters* (Windsor: Biblioasis, 2017), as does Andrew Forbes
in his delightful book, *The Utility of Boredom: Baseball Essays*
(Halifax: Invisible Publishing, 2016). As for fishing and boredom,
please see Kingwell, *Catch and Release: Trout Fishing and the
Meaning of Life* (Toronto: Viking, 2003/4). Neither of these forms
of leisure, despite the anguished cries of a beer-deprived Homer
Simpson at a Springfield-Shelbyville match – "I never realized

how boring this game is!" – strikes me as at all boring. (See "The Simpsons – Baseball's Boring," YouTube, 4 June 2011, https://www.youtube.com/watch?v=VlORWhsJjNM). As a merely casual fan of opera, I can claim no special insight about the boredom some patrons experience at the spectacle; but I will note that, at a Toronto performance of Benjamin Britten's rather long *Death in Venice* (2010), one excited audience member was heard to shout, as the curtain rang down, "Hallelujah, I made it!"

5 Pierre Bourdieu, *Distinction: A Social Critique of the Judgment of Taste*, trans. Richard Nice (Cambridge, MA: Harvard University Press, 1984).

6 I have much more to say about procrastination – of course I do, because I was avoiding doing other things when I wrote it! – in Kingwell, "Meaning to Get To: Procrastination and the Art of Life," *Queen's Quarterly* 109, no. 3 (Fall 2002): 363–81.

7 Some recent examples, with a somewhat wide range of nuance and insight, Andrew Sullivan, "I Used to Be a Human Being," *New York Magazine*, 18 September 2016, http://nymag.com/selectall/2016/09/andrew-sullivan-my-distraction-sickness-and-yours.html; Michael Harris, *Solitude: A Singular Life in a Crowded World* (Toronto: Doubleday, 2017); Anthony Storr, *Solitude: A Return to the Self* (New York: New, 2005); Katrina Onstad, *The Weekend Effect: The Life-Changing Benefits of Taking Time Off and Challenging the Cult of Overwork* (Toronto: HarperCollins, 2017); Witold Rybczynski, *Waiting for the Weekend* (New York: Viking, 1991).

8 Mary Mann, *Yawn: Adventures in Boredom* (New York: FSG Originals, 2017). Mann does not explore a larger intellectual context for her musings, nor does she, despite the high-spirited sound of "adventures" in her subtitle, and chapter headings like "In a Cubicle with the Desert Fathers" and "Bored in Baghdad," actually go anywhere. Barring a trip from New York to Kansas City and various forays from her apartment to her college library, a sex-toy store event, or the local cinema, she doesn't seem to go anywhere. She does interview a wide variety of characters, from scientists to soldiers – they were the ones bored in Baghdad – but these figures come and go like ghosts behind a scrim whose front stage has just one

player. Maybe even more inevitably, we learn of her family history of depression, her easy irritability, and the college boyfriend who cheated on her. (Was he bored?) This is book so relentlessly personal, yet so unilluminating, that I'm tempted to say that the only ideal reader for it is Mary Mann herself, or maybe someone who desperately wants to be her friend. These persons may exist, but I confess I am not one of them.

9 It is of course not the case, as many British (and Canadian) people like to claim, that Americans simply don't "get" irony. It is rather that the context of ironic engagement must be clear – no meta-moves allowed, in other words: you can't be ironic about what is going on. The English poet C. Day Lewis, writing under the pseudonym he adopted for a series of excellent murder mysteries, Nicholas Blake, makes the point. The detective, Nigel Strangeways, is visiting an American college based on Harvard. He marvels at the ability of another visitor, a voluble Irishman, to manage the social conventions: "He had adapted himself to what seemed to Nigel a basic rule of American conversation – one may be serious or frivolous, but never both in the same paragraph." Nicholas Blake, *The Morning after Death* (New York: Harper & Row, 1966), 5.

10 E.H. Gombrich, "Pleasures of Boredom: Four Centuries of Doodles," in Gombrich, *The Uses of Images* (London: Phaidon, 1999), 212–25.

11 E.H. Gombrich, *The Sense of Order: A Study in the Psychology of Decorative Art* (London: Phaidon, 1994).

12 Theodor Adorno, *Minima Moralia: Reflections from a Damaged Life*, trans. E.F.N. Jephcott (New York: Verso, 1974), 25.

13 Tom McDonough, *Boredom* (Cambridge, MA: MIT Press, 2017). This book offers a compelling series of meditations on boredom from contemporary artists and writers, broken up by ingenious graphic treatments.

14 Julian Jason Haladyn, *Boredom and Art: Passions of the Will to Boredom* (Alresford: Zero Books, 2015).

15 Susan Sontag, *As Consciousness Is Harnessed to Flesh: Journals and Notebooks, 1964–1980* (New York: Farrar, Straus & Giroux, 2012); quoted in Maria Popova, "Susan Sontag on the Creative Purpose of Boredom," brainpickings, https://www.brainpickings.org/2012/10/26/susan-sontag-on-boredom/.

16 http://johncage.org/4_33.html.

17 Andy Warhol and Pat Hackett, POPism: *The Warhol '60s* (New York: Hutchinson, 1980), quoted in McDonough, *Boredom*, 70.

18 Georges Perec, *An Attempt at Exhausting a Place in Paris*, trans. Marc Lowenthal (Cambridge, MA: Wakefield, 2010). Perec's choice of intersection to observe was Place Saint-Sulpice, observed obsessively from a variety of café terraces.

19 The Invisible Committee, *The Coming Insurrection* (New York: Semiotext(e), 2009).

20 Manchette's most successful novels are *3 to Kill*, trans. Donald Nicholson-Smith (San Francisco: City Lights, 2002); and *The Prone Gunman*, trans. James Brook (San Francisco: City Lights, 2002). Ballard's *Super-Cannes* (London: Picador, 2002), and Houellebecq's *Elementary Particles*, trans. Frank Wynne (New York: Vintage, 2001) capture the peculiar combination of prosperous boredom and lurking, barely contained violence.

21 Kingwell, *Nearest Thing to Heaven: The Empire State Building and American Dreams* (New Haven: Yale University Press, 2006).

22 Pandora Sykes, "The Rise of the Voice Note, by Pandora Sykes," *Sunday Times*, 8 July 2018, https://www.thetimes.co.uk/article/the-rise-of-the-voice-note-by-pandora-sykes-25shns8rd.

23 Gardiner, "Multitude Strikes Back?," 45.

24 Nadia Kounang, "Watching Cute Cat Videos Is Instinctive and Good for You – Seriously," CNN.com, 20 January 2016, https://www.cnn.com/2016/01/20/health/your-brain-on-cute/index.html.

25 Gardiner, "Multitude Strikes Back?," 46.

26 See, for example, Bruce O'Neill, *The Space of Boredom: Homelessness in the Slowing Global Order* (Durham, NC: Duke University Press, 2017).

27 Mark Kingwell, *Better Living: In Pursuit of Happiness from Plato to Prozac* (Toronto: Viking, 1998); as *In Pursuit of Happiness* (New York: Crown, 2000).

28 Žižek, *Looking Awry*, 69.

29 Louis Althusser, *The Future Lasts Forever*, trans. Richard Veasey (New York: W.W. Norton, 1993).

30 Gilbert Adair, "Getting Away with Murder: It's the Talk of Paris," *Independent*, 2 July 1992, https://www.independent.co.uk/voices/ getting-away-with-murder-its-the-talk-of-paris-how-louis-althusser-killed-his-wife-how-he-was-an-1530755.html.

ANNOTATED BIBLIOGRAPHY

Note: The following bibliography sets out details of some key texts in the study of boredom. Details of specific sources used in the present book, as well as some further contextual material, may be found in the endnotes.

General

Calhoun, Cheshire. "Living with Boredom." *Sophia* 50, no. 2 (2011): 269–79. Calhoun argues that boredom is unavoidable for people who have leisure time because people have a limited capacity to think up ways of filling their time. When people's ingenuity fails they often turn either to purposeless activities (solitaire, surfing the web, etc.) or to harmful activities (gambling, drugs, etc.).

Eastwood, John D., Alexandra Frischen, Mark J. Fenske, and Daniel Smilek. "The Unengaged Mind: Defining Boredom in Terms of Attention." *Perspectives on Psychological Science* 7, no. 5 (2012): 482–95. The authors examine boredom as it relates to attention and propose that boredom has three facets: The inability to engage one's attention with satisfying internal or external stimuli. Focusing one's attention on the fact that one's attention is unengaged. Attributing one's lack of satisfying engagement to the environment.

Elpidorou, Andreas. "The Bright Side of Boredom." *Frontiers in Psychology* 5 (2014): 1245.

Elpidorou argues that boredom is not entirely negative; rather boredom is valuable because it motivates people to abandon unfulfilling situations and seek meaningful activity. Elpidorou argues that without boredom people would remain stuck in unsatisfactory situations and miss out on valuable and satisfying experiences.

– "The Quiet Alarm." *Aeon*, 30 July 2015. https://aeon.co/essays/ life-without-boredom-would-be-a-nightmare.

Elpidorou argues that boredom is significant because it alerts people to the fact that they are caught in an unsatisfactory situation, prompting the subject of boredom to find something more rewarding to do. However, nowadays people cover up the sensation of boredom by scrolling through their smartphones, preventing boredom from doing its job.

– "The Significance of Boredom: A Sartrean Reading." In *Philosophy of Mind and Phenomenology: Conceptual and Empirical Approaches*, edited by Daniel O. Dahlstrom, Andreas Elpidorou, and Walter Hopp, np. New York: Routledge, 2016.

Elpidorou argues that boredom is significant because it alerts people to the fact that they are caught in an unsatisfactory situation, prompting the subject of boredom to find something more rewarding to do.

Raposa, Michael L. *Boredom and the Religious Imagination*. Charlottesville: University of Virginia Press, 1999.

For Raposa the experience of boredom serves paradoxically as both a threat to spiritual life – people find the activities of their religious life uninteresting and disengage – and also as a possible prompt to a search for religious meaning and a deepening of spiritual life.

Svendsen, Lars. *A Philosophy of Boredom*. Translated by John Irons. London: Reaktion, 2005.

Svendsen explores the history of boredom philosophy, focusing particularly on Romanticism and Martin Heidegger. Svendsen himself views boredom as a potential incentive to creativity.

Politics/Social Organization and Boredom

Carroll, B.J., P. Parker, and K. Inkson. "Evasion of Boredom: An Unexpected Spur to Leadership?" *Human Relations* 63, no. 7 (2010): 1031–49.
The authors argue that a proclivity toward boredom may be a characteristic of good leaders because it can be a spur to creative thinking, risk-taking, and flexibility in problem-solving.

Haller, Max, Markus Hadler, and Gerd Kaup. "Leisure Time in Modern Societies: A New Source of Boredom and Stress?" *Social Indicators Research* 111, no. 2 (2012): 403–34.
This study analyzes the ISSP-2007 survey on leisure time and finds that approximately 60 per cent of people surveyed feel that they do not have enough leisure time and approximately 33 per cent of people felt bored in their free time.

Kustermans, Jorg, and Erik Ringmar. "Modernity, Boredom, and War: A Suggestive Essay." *Review of International Studies* 37, no. 4 (2010): 1775–92.
The authors posit that both the search for world peace and the sensation of boredom are characteristics of the modern world. The authors argue that as the Western world becomes more peaceful and boredom increases, people turn increasingly to representations of violence and the glorification of war for stimulation.

Tilburg, Wijnand A.P. Van, and Eric R. Igou. "Going to Political Extremes in Response to Boredom." *European Journal of Social Psychology* 46, no. 6 (2016): 687–99.

The authors conclude that there is a relationship between boredom and "extreme political orientation" because boredom drives people to seek alternate sources of meaning in their lives.

Boredom and Technology

Panova, Tayana, and Alejandro Lleras. "Avoidance or Boredom: Negative Mental Health Outcomes Associated with Use of Information and Communication Technologies Depend on Users' Motivations." *Computers in Human Behavior* 58 (2016): 249–58.
The authors found that using technology to alleviate boredom was not linked to higher rates of depression and anxiety amongst users. However, using technology to cope with anxiety over the long term could have a "negative influence on mental health."

Skues, Jason, Ben Williams, Julian Oldmeadow, and Lisa Wise. "The Effects of Boredom, Loneliness, and Distress Tolerance on Problem Internet Use among University Students." *International Journal of Mental Health and Addiction* 14, no. 2 (2015): 167–80.
This study examined the internet use habits of 169 undergraduates and concluded the boredom-prone students tended to turn to the internet in search of stimulus. Their excessive internet use led in turn to poorer academic results.

Thiele, Leslie Paul. "Postmodernity and the Routinization of Novelty: Heidegger on Boredom and Technology." *Polity* 29, no. 4 (1997): 489–517.
This study examines Heidegger's view that the modern world's obsession with constant technological innovation and advancement is driven by our "profound boredom." But by turning to technological novelties to mask our boredom we skirt our responsibility to find our place in the world.

Psychological States and Boredom

Barnett, Lynn A., and Sandra Wolf Klitzing. "Boredom in Free Time: Relationships with Personality, Affect, and Motivation for Different Gender, Racial and Ethnic Student Groups." *Leisure Sciences* 28, no. 3 (2006): 223–44.

In this study a questionnaire was administered to 999 university students. The results were used to describe the "group's similarities and differences" of students prone to being bored in their free time. The study revealed that race, ethnicity, and gender are the only "significant demographic predictors" of boredom proneness.

Fahlman, Shelley A., Kimberley B. Mercer, Peter Gaskovski, Adrienne E. Eastwood, and John D. Eastwood. "Does a Lack of Life Meaning Cause Boredom? Results from Psychometric, Longitudinal, and Experimental Analyses." *Journal of Social and Clinical Psychology* 28, no. 3 (2009): 307–40.

This study examines the correlation between "life meaning," depression and anxiety, and boredom. In brief the results demonstrated that "life meaning" and boredom are much more strongly correlated than depression or anxiety and boredom.

Hendricks, Gaironeesa, Shazly Savahl, and Maria Florence. "Adolescent Peer Pressure, Leisure Boredom, and Substance Use in Low-Income Cape Town Communities." *Social Behavior and Personality: An International Journal* 44, no. 3 (2016): 99–109.

This study concludes that while both boredom and peer pressure predicted substance use in the community under investigation, peer pressure was the more significant predictor of the two.

INDEX

Page numbers in italics refer to illustrations

transitive boredom, 18

Trump, Donald: censorship, 83–4; civility, 78; EU Google fine, 115–16; net neutrality and, 111–12; not the first, 69, 74–5; nuclear weapons, 75–6; post-truth condition, 58–60, 67–8; Twitter, 79–80. *See also* post-truth condition

truth: algorithms, 61; limits of speaking truth to power, 94–5; ministerial and magisterial reason, 61; subjectivism, objectivism, and contextualism, 68–74. *See also* post-truth condition

TTYL!, 142

Turner's sunset, 26, 125–6

Twitter, 75, 79, 88. *See also* Interface

uncanny, 98, 141

urban design, 121–2

US Federal Communications Commission (FCC), 111

US Federal Trade Commission (FTC), 116

US presidential elections, 2016, 105–6, 108

vampires, 60, 62, 63

van Zuylen, Marina, 159n53

Veblen, Thorstein, 43, 134

Verizon, 111, 114

Vestager, Margrethe, 115

Vicious Circle of Boredom, 29, 31

Virilio, Paul, 127

virtue ethic, 77

waiting: learning to wait, 29–32, 146, 147; psychoanalytic boredom, 35–6; in train stations, xii, 16–17, 21

Waldron, Jeremy, 110

Wallace, David Foster, 44, 124–5

WALL-E (film), 128

war: ever-present conditions of, 56–7

Warhol, Andy, 140; *Empire,* 141

Waugh, Evelyn, 19

well-being, boredom as, xii

Welsh, Irvine *(Trainspotting),* 50

Wenders, Wim *(Wings of Desire),* 142

Wharton, Edith, 43

"What Is Enlightenment?" (Kant), 71

Wheeler, Tom, 111

Williamson, Timothy: *The Philosophy of Philosophy,* 30, 158n50

Wings of Desire (film), 142

Wittgenstein, Ludwig, 10

women's experience of boredom, 154–5n1

wonder, 155n3; affinity to boredom, 8, 9

Woolworth Building, New York (postcard, 1912), vi, x

word-casings, 36–7; technology, 44

work: free time, 24–6, 27, 28–9, 37–40; self-consumption and the Interface, 6–8, 52–3, 126–9; shifting notions of, 7–8

World as Will and Representation, The (Schopenhauer), 12

Young, Edward: *Night-Thoughts,* 51

Zen Buddhist thought, 138

Žižek, Slavoj, 36, 44, 147, 153–4n4

Zuckerberg, Mark, 105, 169–70n5